THE COMPLETE BOOK OF

PASTA SAUCES

THE BEST ITALIAN
Pestos, Marinaras, Ragùs,
and Other Cooked and Fresh Sauces
for Every Type of Pasta Imaginable

ALLAN BAY

HARVARD
COMMON
PRESS

Inspiring | Educating | Creating | Entertaining

Brimming with creative inspiration, how-to projects, and useful information to enrich your everyday life, Quarto.com is a favorite destination for those pursuing their interests and passions.

© 2022 Quarto Publishing Group USA Inc.
Text © 2022 Giunti Editore S.p.A., Firenze-Milano

English edition first published in 2022 by The Harvard Common Press,
an imprint of The Quarto Group,
100 Cummings Center, Suite 265-D, Beverly, MA 01915, USA.
T (978) 282-9590 F (978) 283-2742 Quarto.com

The Harvard Common Press titles are also available at discount for retail, wholesale, promotional, and bulk purchase. For details, contact the Special Sales Manager by email at specialsales@quarto.com or by mail at The Quarto Group, Attn: Special Sales Manager, 100 Cummings Center, Suite 265-D, Beverly, MA 01915, USA.

26 25 24 23 22   1 2 3 4 5

ISBN: 978-0-7603-7647-8

Digital edition published in 2022
eISBN: 978-0-7603-7648-5

Library of Congress
Cataloging-in-Publication Data
is available.

DESIGN: Cindy Samargia Laun
COVER IMAGE: Shutterstock
PAGE LAYOUT: Cindy Samargia Laun
PHOTOGRAPHY: Shutterstock

Originally published as
Il Libro Completo dei Sughi, delle Salse e dei Ragù.
Copyright © 2016 by Giunti Editore S.p.A.,
Firenze-Milano
www.giunti.it

GRAPHIC DESIGN: Raffaele Anello
COVER: Raffaele Anello, Lorenzo Pacini
EDITOR: Micaela Vissani
LAYOUT AND EDITING: Studio Newt, Florence
TRANSLATION: Kosmos
HEAD OF FOOD AND WINE DEPARTMENT: Marco Bolasco

Printed in China

The author would like to thank Shamira Gatta and Manuela Vanni for their collaboration.

CONTENTS

INTRODUCTION

Paraphrasing Goethe's famous line, "Kennst du das Land, wo die Zitronen blühn, . . ." (Do you know the land where lemon trees blossom, . . .), I can say that Italy is the land where sauces blossom.

But, what is a sauce? It is a preparation that serves to enhance a base, usually a starch, such as bread, pasta, polenta, potatoes, rice, and the like, but also many other dishes. This base is also elevated if the sauce is added in a small dose, therefore at a limited cost: a clever, logical, and economical thing to do.

What would a dish be if not topped with a sauce? Compare a slice of bread with bruschetta, or contrast a plain polenta dish with one enhanced with fresh herbs—a staple dish of Italians for centuries—and you will immediately understand the difference.

A sauce, too, is typically Italian, because Italians have always been devout starch eaters, and so we put all our creativity, a virtue which, fortunately, we do not lack, into enriching the starch creatively, and at a low cost.

Abroad, especially in England, France, and Germany, you'll find few sauces, but many gravies. These gravies are generally made with the discards (bones, vegetable scraps, etc.,) of the main dish ingredients they are meant to enhance, or with the cooking juices of that dish almost always thickened with butter, cream, or flour. So, we can see these gravies, versus sauces, are created to enrich a protein base, such as beef, pork, poultry, or seafood—a completely different origin and use.

That said, the distinction between sauce and gravy today, when we all eat better, lighter, has blurred. Sauces have become richer and more varied, thanks also to the discovery of other people's traditional sauces that we have made our own and that now belong to everyone, and gravies have become lighter and more eclectic.

So, we can really call any preparation that serves to enrich a dish a "sauce," whatever it may be. If we want to subdivide this category, we can define "ragù" as a partially creamy sauce made with ingredients cut into pieces; a "sauce" as a blended condiment, and a "pesto" when the ingredients have been pounded and blended. It is also fair to refer to preparations such as mayonnaise, rouille, sour cream, or stocks as "sauces," which, so far, no one has done.

I know that many will disagree with this partition of mine and some will be horrified to see something they have always called "gravy" referred to as "sauce," or vice versa. But I am a lifelong cataloger, who considers the "Catalogue of Ships" in the second book of Homer's *Iliad*, where the contingents of the Achaean armies that arrived at Troy are listed, to be a poem. Many say it is only a list of names. For me, and for catalogers like me, there is just as much pathos in those verses as in those of the wrath of Achilles . . . I know that by cataloging something one must sometimes force it, but I also know that one cannot write about cooking if one does not dare to categorize.

I have always been a serial sauceophile: I can't conceive of any preparation that isn't topped with an appropriate sauce. Over the years, I have dedicated more time to the study of sauces than to any other subject in the kitchen. For years, I have had this book in my head, where the highlight of the recipe is the sauce and then, but only as a consequence, you'll find a suggestion for where it can be used. For so many reasons, the book was never written. Today, it is finally here.

As for the title, which is a very important thing for a book, I had no idea. The structure of the book was clear to me, but how to best summarize it in a few words was not. Then, one day I got a call from the publisher telling me that during one of those long meetings that punctuate the routine of publishing houses, the salespeople had suggested *The Interpretation of Sauces*—a tribute, rightly ironic, to the mythical *The Interpretation of Dreams* by Sigmund Freud. I liked it instantly, and I still do.

So, here is my repertoire of almost 200 sauces and their suggested base pairings, with the hope that they can always enrich your table and your beloved dishes!

—Allan Bay

READER'S GUIDE

This book includes nearly 200 recipes for pestos, ragùs, sauces, and other similar preparations describing how to prepare them. These sauces are usually savory, but sweet sauces are also included, intended to be used on savory preparations. For sweet dishes, we will see, in the future . . .

The amounts given only indicate the balance among the ingredients used, with a recommendation for the number of servings they will yield, depending on how you use it and appetites at the table. You might use just one spoonful in a soup or on a crostini, or add the whole thing to a beautiful bowl of pasta, so the number of servings may vary. Feel free to increase quantities, keeping the ratios the same, to suit your needs.

Many recipes include diced onion, celery, and carrot—a cornerstone of good Italian cooking. Sometimes, however, a recipe will call for "soffrito" (sautéed minced vegetables) and the three classic vegetables (onion, celery, carrot) separately. This is because they serve different purposes. Classically, the diced vegetables add flavor. The soffrito, which is basically a blend of these diced vegetables that is sautéed, helps thicken the sauce, giving it the right body and (creamy) texture. Note, too, that cream, tomatoes, and vegetable purées are used as thickeners (you will see them often). Unblended sauces are always thickened by blending about half of the sauce and then incorporating it into the unblended portion. This process is essential for best results.

You can make soffrito ahead in large batches and keep it refrigerated in an airtight container or jar, or freeze as "cubes." (One cube generally equals about 1 ounce [28 g], or 2 tablespoons [30 ml].) Put the soffrito in warmed silicone ice-cube molds placed on a baking sheet to help keep the shape, put the tray with the molds in the freezer. The next day remove the cubes from the mold, place them in a resealable freezer bag, and keep frozen for up to 3 months, using them as needed (in many cases you can just add the frozen cubes to the sauce).

SOFFRITO

- 2 medium yellow onions, peeled and finely chopped
- 1 celery rib, finely chopped
- 1 large carrot, peeled and finely chopped
- ¼ cup (60 ml) olive oil

1. Sauté the vegetables quite slowly over low heat in a skillet or saucepan, stirring frequently, until they just begin to turn brown and caramelize, about 20 minutes.

Yield: Makes about 2 cups (260 g)

THE BEST COMBINATIONS

Following are the base recommendations you'll find mixed and matched with the sauce recipes for good pairings, and some tips on how to add the sauce to the dish. "Best on:" listings in a recipe are the optimal matches for a particular sauce and base— a perfect union!

COOKED PASTA

There are a few ways to dress cooked pasta with sauce.

AL DENTE PASTA WITH COOKED SAUCE

This is the most classic method of cooking and saucing pasta, including egg pastas. Cook the sauce in a saucepan or a skillet big enough to hold the pasta, with a wide base and sloping sides (in Italian, this pan does not have a precise name; in French, it is a *sauteuse*). Cook the pasta in another pot, preferably one made of stainless steel, in abundant water—at least 4 cups (960 ml) water per 4 ounces (115 g) of pasta (more is better)—salted when it boils, stirring gently, until al dente. Drain the pasta, reserving a little (about ½ cup, or 120 ml, for 4 servings) of the cooking water. Add the pasta to the sauce and gently toss it to coat and combine. Cook over high heat for 1 to 2 minutes, tossing, and adding the cooking water a little at a time, and other finishing ingredients, such as parsley.

If you would like to add a little fat, such as butter, add it cold from the refrigerator with the heat turned off. Also, the classic addition of grated cheese should be done with the heat off.

PARTIALLY COOKED PASTA WITH COOKED SAUCE (RISOTTO STYLE)

This technique of combining cooked pasta with a cooked sauce allows the pasta to absorb, in part, the liquid part of the sauce, which delivers a creamier result, as the pasta releases some of its starch as it finished cooking. Cook the pasta in plenty of boiling salted water until about two-thirds done, or a bit more or less, as you prefer. Drain the pasta, reserving some of the cooking water (about 2 cups, or 480 ml, per 8 ounces, or 225 g, of pasta cooked), and toss the pasta in the pan with the sauce. Finish cooking the pasta risotto-style, stirring and adding the cooking water little by little, adding more water only after the previous amount has been absorbed. This method takes a few minutes longer than the traditional saucing of al dente pasta. Add any fat or cheese at the end, with the heat off. This method is not recommended for egg pastas.

AL DENTE PASTA WITH UNCOOKED SAUCE

Cook the pasta as described in Al Dente Pasta with Cooked Sauce (see this page), drain it, toss the hot pasta in a bowl containing the uncooked sauce, such as a pesto, stir it, add a little fat and cheese if desired, and serve. *Follow this procedure only if you are using an uncooked sauce*, which does not stand up to cooking. This method also works well with egg pastas.

PASTA SALAD

The problem with pasta salad is how to best cool the cooked pasta after draining it. I recommend draining the cooked pasta, passing it under cool running water for no more than a few seconds, draining it again well, and placing it in a large bowl. Dress the cooled pasta with oil or another fat, stir, and let rest for at least 20 minutes, stirring from time to time, before dressing it with a room-temperature sauce. Do not refrigerate, as the salad will not hold up well.

LAYERED AND STUFFED PASTA

LASAGNA AND CANNELLONI
Use the sauce to stuff or top cannelloni or between layers of lasagna noodles before baking, along with béchamel to taste, grated or shredded cheeses, fats, and other ingredients as desired.

STUFFED PASTA
Whether stuffed with cheese, meat, seafood, or vegetables, stuffed pastas (meaning completely sealed, which is why cannelloni is excluded from this category) and egg pastas, such as ravioli, should be tossed with a sauce. Choose a sauce that complements the filling and don't be afraid to experiment. I once made pork-filled ravioli with a clam sauce (a sort of surf and turf), an East Asian tradition, that worked deliciously.

RICE DISHES

RICE

We call recipes using a traditional Italian rice, a round variety, cooked in boiling water, either by absorption, that is, when it is cooked until all the liquid has been absorbed by the rice, or by draining the rice once cooked, "rice of" or "rice with." In the first case, proceed exactly as with risotto (see this page); in the second case, drain the rice and dress it in a bowl with the sauce, adding cheese and other ingredients off the heat.

When making a rice salad, the same principles for making a pasta salad (see page 12) apply, maybe even more so: Cooling the rice under running water causes it to become too waterlogged, so using a long-grain rice, parboiled rice, black, brown, red, or other type of rice, can be the solution. Or, use a pasta called risone, also known as orzo, which is shaped like grains of rice. Dress the cooked rice with a warm sauce, or sauté it for a minute in the saucepan with the sauce.

RISOTTO

Risotto is made by toasting rice in a saucepan without added fat over medium-high heat for a couple of minutes, stirring, and then simmering it in a liquid (in principle, a broth consistent with the sauce), added a little at a time, by the ladleful (about ½ cup, or 120 ml), until the rice fully absorbs the liquid and releases its starches as it cook. It is the initial toasting that turns a rice into a risotto—without the toasting, the dish is simply rice.

One minute before the risotto is ready, add the sauce, cooked to perfection. Stir, adjust the salt, and *mantecate*, which means to add 1½ tablespoons (21 g) of cold butter and mix well. Instead of butter, oils, such as hazelnut and walnut, can be used, and in some cases, even extra-virgin olive oil, but use a light one. Then, add cheese if desired, stir, cover, let stand for a couple of minutes, and serve.

As is often the case in cooking, there is an exception: if you use rice that has been aged for a year or more, which is fashionable today, you do not need to toast it. The aging process replaces the toasting, but the dish is called risotto all the same. Start cooking the rice with 1 cup (240 ml) of boiling broth and bring it to a simmer.

OTHER STARCHES AND LEGUMES

BOILED POTATOES

This is a simple procedure. Wash the potatoes and cook them in water (steaming is preferable; it takes the same amount of time as boiling). Drain the potatoes, or remove them from the steamer, peel, if you wish (I never peel them), halve them, and top with a warm sauce. Cooked potatoes pair deliciously with almost any sauce in this book, which is no small feat.

BRUSCHETTA AND CROSTINI

When serving bruschetta or crostini, slices of toasted bread (from the toaster or oven), serve hot bruschetta or crostini with a warm sauce and cold bruschetta and crostini with a cold sauce.

CRESPELLE

The French call them crêpes. You can make your own crespelle, or buy them. Place the crespelle, whether hot, warm, or at room temperature, on a work surface and evenly distribute the sauce over them. Fold the crespelle into the shape of an omelet or roll them up, place in a baking pan brushed with butter or another fat, cover them, if you wish, with a little béchamel, and bake in a 400°F (200°C, or gas mark 6) oven for 10 minutes until browned and bubbling.

GNOCCHI

In Italy, gnocchi are made mainly of potatoes, but they can also be made with vegetables and flour, chestnuts, legumes, polenta, ricotta, or other ingredients. Just as with pasta, you want to imbue the cooked gnocchi with flavor from the sauce. Using a slotted spoon, transfer the boiled gnocchi as soon as they come to the surface of the water into the pan with the warm sauce and cook for 1 minute over medium heat, stirring gently.

POLENTA

The simplest procedure: Top a hot slice of polenta with a warm sauce; even simpler: mix the polenta with the warm sauce in the dish. You can also add the sauce to the polenta during the last 2 minutes of cooking. In any case, a sauce should always be added, even enhancing it with a fat.

PIZZA, FOCACCIA, PIADINA

For pizza, remove the crust from the oven 2 minutes before it is ready. Spread the sauce over the crust and bake for 2 minutes more until the crust is browned and the sauce is hot. Use the same method for focaccia, or halve the loaf horizontally, spread the sauce on the bottom half, top with the remaining half, and bake for 2 minutes. For piadina (flatbread), stuff it with a warm sauce when it is nice and hot, or cold, and serve.

STEWED LEGUMES

Put the cooked legumes, either at room temperature or hot, in a bowl and stir in the chosen sauce. Taste and adjust the salt, if needed, and season with oil and vinegar, if desired. You can never go wrong by adding a touch of mustard.

MEATS AND SEAFOOD

COOKED MEATS

Cold cooked meats, whether boiled, grilled, roasted, or cooked other ways, cut as thick or thin as you like, are typically topped with ketchup or mayonnaise. You can, instead, top them with a sauce or two of your choice, warm, slightly chilled, or at room temperature and, if you wish, drizzle with a splash of oil.

Some sauces are more suitable for hot roasts, boiled meats, stews, and so on, whether sliced or diced. They're also great with leftover meats, cut thick or thin as you like, and reheated by baking, microwaving, pan-frying, or steaming, then topped with your sauces, hot or lukewarm, of choice, and drizzled with oil, if you wish.

COOKED FISH

Cold fish fillets, cooked quickly (so it is not carpaccio) can be served with slightly chilled or room-temperature sauces and drizzled with a little oil, if desired.

Hot fish fillets, or whole fish, boiled, grilled, or baked, can be served with a sauce of choice, hot or warm, and a splash of oil, if you like.

RAW MEAT AND FISH: TARTARES AND CARPACCIOS

Tartares are preparations of ground raw meat or fish, whereas *carpaccios* are thinly sliced raw meat or fish. To prepare a tartare, dice the meat with a little patience—if you grind it with a meat grinder, the meat will become too crumbly. For a carpaccio, the slices must be very thin. Although cutting the meat by hand can be difficult, you can freeze the protein for about 30 minutes before slicing to make cutting it easier. Dress either preparation with a room-temperature sauce and, if you wish, a touch of oil.

CRUSTACEANS

Shrimp, langoustines, or crawfish, but also lobster meat cut into chunks, served raw or blanched or sautéed for a minute, can be topped with a sauce of choice, hot or warm, and a drizzle of oil.

OTHER BASES

COOKED VEGETABLES

However you cook them, vegetables are easily enhanced with a spoonful of warm sauce. If vegetables are served cold, the sauce should be at slightly chilled or at room temperature.

EGGS

Whether hard-boiled, poached, scrambled, or made into omelets, a spoonful of a warm sauce is a welcome topping for any type of cooked eggs. If serving hard-boiled eggs cold, use a room-temperature sauce.

VELOUTÉS AND CREAM SOUPS

Every velouté and cream soup is greatly enriched, even aesthetically, when topped with a spoonful of a complementary sauce. Just put the sauce, warm or even room temperature, in the center of the serving bowl.

A SHORT GLOSSARY

EQUIPMENT

Following is some of the most commonly used equipment you'll find in the book.

A **pot** is a cylindrical cooking vessel, preferably made of stainless steel, with a height greater than its diameter. It is mainly used for boiling pasta and preparing broths. A **small pot** is a small, cylindrical, one-handled container used to heat liquids.

A **saucepan** is a cylindrical cooking vessel with a height smaller than its diameter and that can be made from a variety of materials, especially stainless steel and aluminum. It is a universal cooking vessel that is a good choice for preparing 90 percent or more of the dishes here.

A **skillet** is a low cooking container with curved sides and a handle. It is used for sautéing and frying as well as making sauces. If the sides are higher and flared, the pan is called a sauteuse, and is perfect for sautéing.

INGREDIENTS

Following are some tips regarding ingredients used in the recipes.

"Cream" means fresh heavy whipping cream. I do not demonize other creams, but they should not be used.

With some exceptions, **grana**, without further specifying, is used to indicate a grated cheese, usually a hard cheese with a granular texture. Use what you have on hand or prefer, whether Asiago, Grana Padano, Parmigiano-Reggiano, Pecorino Romano, or other.

"Olive oil" means extra-virgin olive oil unless otherwise specified. Generally speaking, if it is used during cooking it must be delicate, such as a Ligurian or Garda olive oil; if it is added at the end of cooking it can be flavorful. How much you use depends on the dish being made and your taste. I would suggest that the oil never be too strongly flavored.

Seasonings: **Salt** should be added in small quantities and according to your taste at the end of cooking, with some exceptions. **Pepper** should also be added at the end of cooking, grinding it fresh just as much as possible. **Spices**, too, should be added at the end of cooking: Some spices are thermolabile, meaning they are degraded in nutrients and flavor by the heat of cooking and, so, are best used as a garnish or stirred into the food just before serving.

When **spinach** is called for in a recipe, use fresh spinach in season for best results.

"Sugar" means granulated sugar unless otherwise specified.

Tomatoes are used often—they represent Italy's national flavor. However, I rarely specify which type of tomato to use—in my opinion, as long as they are good, the sauce will be delicious. Use whatever kind of tomatoes you prefer or have available, making sure to choose ripe, but not soft, ones. Keep tomatoes at room temperature, not in the refrigerator (the cold temperature slows their maturation and changes the texture).

Vinegar always means red wine vinegar. If white or made of other ingredients, such as apple cider vinegar, it is specified.

The **weight of peas and beans** refers to the shelled product.

Whenever **wine** is added to a sauce, simmer it for 3 minutes so the alcohol, about 12 percent in wine, evaporates. Alcohol that is not evaporated can give a bitter taste to the dish. In some cases, this is specified, but it is best if you always evaporate the wine. If you don't want to cook with wine, substitute an equal amount of an appropriate broth or water.

Yogurt must be whole milk, and if it's Greek, therefore firm and flavorful, it's better. Much better. Using low-fat yogurt . . . I don't see why you would.

TECHNIQUE

Following are some tips regarding techniques and instructions used in the recipes.

When **baking in the oven**, the oven should be preheated and at the specified temperature when the food is put into it.

"Cook" means to cook on the stovetop, uncovered, without a lid. If the pan or other cooking vessel should be covered with a lid, the recipe specifies it.

To **cut into julienne** means to prepare an ingredient by cutting it into very thin sticks or slices.

Cut into strips means to cut an ingredient to a minimal thickness, but with a width of up to ½ inch (1 cm).

Deglazing a pan is done by adding a liquid, usually wine, and letting it evaporate, while stirring and scraping up any browned bits from the bottom of the pan to incorporate all the flavor.

To top means to put a sauce on top of a base ingredient for serving.

1
HEALTHY AND VIBRANT
VEGETABLE
SAUCES

ASPARAGUS AND ALMOND SAUCE

Yield: 4 servings

1 pound (454 g) asparagus, chopped

Olive oil

1 garlic clove, unpeeled

½ cup (55 g) almonds, coarsely chopped

½ cup (50 g) grated Pecorino Romano cheese

Salt and fresh-cracked black pepper

BEST ON:
- Al dente pasta
- Gnocchi
- Rice and risotto
- Veloutés and cream soups

GOES WELL ON:
- Bruschetta and crostini
- Cooked meats and fish (hot or cold)
- Cooked vegetables
- Crespelle
- Eggs
- Pasta salad
- Raw meats and fish: tartare and carpaccio

1. Pour a few swirls of oil into a skillet and add the garlic clove and asparagus. Sauté over medium heat for 30 seconds to 1 minute until fragrant. Pour in just enough water to cover and bring to a simmer.

2. Remove and discard the garlic and transfer the asparagus mixture to a food processor or blender, or use an immersion blender, and blend until smooth.

3. Add the almonds and cheese. Blend again, adding a little oil, until you have a smooth purée.

4. Taste and season with salt and pepper.

ASPARAGUS AND PINE NUT SAUCE

Yield: 4 to 6 servings

½ cup (70 g) pine nuts

1 pound (454 g) asparagus, peeled and chopped with tips set aside

Olive oil

1 garlic clove, unpeeled

2 tablespoons (20 g) Soffrito (page 11)

Salt and fresh-cracked black pepper

BEST ON:
- Al dente pasta (especially egg pasta)
- Pasta salad
- Gnocchi
- Veloutés and cream soups

GOES WELL ON:
- Cooked meats and fish (hot or cold)
- Cooked vegetables
- Crespelle
- Crustaceans
- Eggs
- Rice and risotto
- Stuffed pasta (cheese, meat, seafood, or vegetables)

1. In a small nonstick skillet over medium-high heat, toast the pine nuts for 2 to 3 minutes until lightly browned and fragrant. Set aside.

2. Pour a few swirls of oil into a skillet and add the unpeeled garlic clove, asparagus stalk pieces, and soffrito. Sauté over medium heat for 30 seconds to 1 minute until fragrant. Pour in just enough water to cover and bring to a simmer.

3. Remove and discard the garlic and transfer the asparagus mixture to a food processor or blender, or use an immersion blender, and blend until smooth. Return the asparagus mixture to medium heat.

4. Halve the asparagus tips lengthwise, add them to the skillet, and cook for about 1 minute until crisp-tender.

5. Taste and season the sauce with salt and pepper and stir in the pine nuts.

BURGUNDY SAUCE

1. In a large skillet over medium heat, melt the butter. Add the onion, mushrooms, bay leaves, thyme, and rosemary and cook for 10 minutes, stirring occasionally, until softened and beginning to brown.

2. Pour in the wine to deglaze the skillet, scraping up any browned bits from the bottom. Simmer for about 3 minutes until the wine evaporates.

3. Sprinkle the mixture with the cornstarch, stir in the soffrito and water, and cook, uncovered, for 15 minutes until the sauce is thickened and hot. Remove and discard the bay leaves, thyme, and rosemary.

4. Taste and season with salt and pepper.

Yield: 4 servings

5½ tablespoons (½ stick plus 1½ tablespoons, or 77 g) butter

1 large white onion, finely diced

About 5 ounces (140 g) champignon (white button) mushrooms, coarsely chopped

2 bay leaves

1 thyme sprig

1 rosemary sprig

½ cup (120 ml) red wine (preferably Burgundy)

2 tablespoons (16 g) cornstarch

¼ cup (33 g) Soffrito (page 11)

1 cup (240 ml) water, plus more as needed

Salt and fresh-cracked black pepper

BEST ON:
- Cooked beef (hot)
- Cooked pasta (all types)

GOES WELL ON:
- Boiled potatoes
- Cooked vegetables
- Crespelle

- Crustaceans
- Gnocchi
- Lasagna and cannelloni
- Polenta
- Rice and risotto
- Stew
- Stuffed pasta (cheese, meat, seafood, or vegetables)

VEGETABLE CARBONARA

Yield: 4 to 6 servings

1 pound (454 g) vegetables
   of choice, diced

Olive oil

5 large egg yolks

½ cup (50 g) grated
   grana (such as Asiago,
   Parmigiano-Reggiano,
   or Pecorino Romano)

Fresh-cracked black pepper

BEST ON:
- Al dente pasta

GOES WELL ON:
- Gnocchi

1. Place the vegetables in a skillet with a few swirls of oil. Sauté over high heat for 3 to 5 minutes, or until soft (depending on the vegetables you use).

2. Transfer half of the cooked vegetables to a food processor or blender, or use an immersion blender. Add about 1 tablespoon (15 ml) of oil and blend until smooth, adding more oil as needed.

3. In a large bowl, whisk the egg yolks while adding the cheese a bit at a time until blended and combined.

4. Generously season with pepper and whisk to combine.

5. When dressing the hot pasta with the sauce, which will cook the eggs gently from its residual heat, add about ½ cup (120 ml) of the pasta cooking water as needed for a creamier texture, along with the puréed vegetables and remaining sautéed vegetables and stir gently to coat and combine. If you're concerned about uncooked egg, combine everything in the skillet and cook gently over low heat for about 1 minute, stirring constantly, to cook the egg.

ARTICHOKE SAUCE

1. Fill a large bowl with water and stir in the lemon juice.

2. Cut off the stems from the artichokes, peel them, and cut the stems into thin slices. Soak the stems in the acidulated lemon water until ready to use.

3. Remove the outer leaves from the artichokes and cut off the tips. Halve the artichokes, then quarter them. Remove the barbs and cut the quarters into pieces. Add them to the lemon water.

4. Pour a few swirls of oil into a nonstick skillet and add the garlic. Sauté over medium heat for about 30 seconds until fragrant.

5. Drain the artichokes and add them to the skillet. Pour in the broth, turn the heat to low, and simmer until tender. Transfer half of the artichokes to a food processor or blender, or to a medium-size bowl and use an immersion blender, and blend until smooth. Stir the purée into the artichokes remaining in the skillet.

6. Taste and season with salt and pepper, then sprinkle with plenty of chopped parsley.

Yield: 4 servings

Juice of 1 lemon

6 artichokes

Olive oil

2 garlic cloves, peeled and finely chopped

1 cup (240 ml) vegetable broth

Salt and fresh-cracked black pepper

1 bunch fresh parsley, finely chopped

BEST ON:
- Bruschetta and crostini
- Cooked pasta (any type)
- Stuffed pasta (cheese, meat, seafood, or vegetables)

GOES WELL ON:
- Cooked meats and fish (hot or cold)
- Cooked vegetables
- Crespelle
- Gnocchi
- Lasagna and cannelloni
- Pasta salad
- Raw meats and fish: tartare and carpaccio
- Rice and risotto
- Veloutés and cream soups

CHESTNUT SAUCE

Yield: 4 servings

1 pound (454 g) chestnuts

7 tablespoons (98 g) butter

¾ cup (102 g) pine nuts

¼ cup (60 ml) brandy

1 bunch fresh wild fennel
    fronds, or fronds from
    1 or 2 fennel bulbs,
    finely chopped

Salt and fresh-cracked
    black pepper

BEST ON:
- Cooked meats
  (hot; such as beef filet,
  ham, or turkey)
- Stuffed pasta (meat)

GOES WELL ON:
- Cooked fish (hot)
- Cooked vegetables
- Crustaceans
- Pizza, focaccia, piadina
- Stuffed pasta (cheese,
  seafood, or vegetables)

1. Using the tip of a sharp knife, score the chestnuts with an X on the bottom.

2. Bring a large pot of salted water to a boil, add the chestnuts, and cook for about 40 minutes until the chestnuts are soft. Drain the chestnuts, reserving 1 cup (240 ml) of the cooking water, let cool slightly, then remove them from their shells and skins. Transfer half of the chestnuts to a food processor or blender, or a medium-size bowl and use an immersion blender, add a splash of the reserved cooking water, and blend until smooth, adding more water as needed.

3. Coarsely chop the remaining chestnuts.

4. In a skillet over medium heat, melt the butter. Toss in the pine nuts and add the chopped chestnuts, then carefully pour in the brandy. Cook for about 3 minutes until the nuts are fragrant and the brandy evaporates.

5. Stir the chopped wild fennel fronds into the skillet, along with the chestnut purée.

6. Taste and season with salt and pepper.

CAULIFLOWER SAUCE

1. In a large saucepan over medium heat, melt the butter.

2. Add the cauliflower and cook for 5 to 8 minutes until the cauliflower begins to soften and brown.

3. Sprinkle the baking soda over the cauliflower, pour in the vegetable broth, and bring the mixture to a boil (it will take about 20 minutes).

4. Transfer the contents of the pan to a food processor or blender, or use an immersion blender, and blend until smooth. Return the sauce to the pan.

5. Taste and season with salt and pepper. Turn the heat to low and simmer to thicken as desired.

Yield: 6 to 8 servings

7 tablespoons (98 g) butter

1 (about 2-pound, or 908 g) head cauliflower, finely chopped

1 tablespoon (14 g) baking soda

2 cups (480 ml) vegetable broth

Salt and fresh-cracked black pepper

BEST ON:
- Al dente pasta
- Cooked vegetables
- Grilled meats

GOES WELL ON:
- Cooked meats and fish (hot or cold)
- Raw meats and fish: tartare and carpaccio
- Rice and risotto
- Stuffed pasta (cheese, meat, seafood, or vegetables)

BROCCOLI RABE SAUCE

Yield: 4 to 6 servings

2 pounds (908 g) broccoli rabe (cime di rapa)

6 salt-packed anchovies

Olive oil

1 garlic clove, peeled and minced

1 fresh chile pepper (such as serrano or jalapeño), destemmed, seeded and minced

Salt and fresh-cracked black pepper

BEST ON:
- Cooked pasta (all types)
- Rice and risotto

GOES WELL ON:
- Cooked meats and fish (hot or cold)
- Cooked vegetables
- Crespelle
- Gnocchi
- Pasta salad
- Polenta
- Rice salad
- Stuffed pasta (cheese, meat, seafood, or vegetables)

1. Clean the broccoli rabe by removing the outer stems and detaching the tops. Mince the inner part of the tops and chop the rest.

2. Remove any bones, heads, and tails from the anchovies and rinse them under running water, then place them in a skillet. Pour in a few swirls of oil and add the chopped broccoli rabe, garlic, and chile pepper. Cook over medium heat for about 3 minutes, stirring frequently, until the vegetables begin to soften and the anchovies dissolve.

3. Stir in the minced broccoli rabe tops and cook for about 5 minutes, stirring, until softened.

4. Taste and season with salt and pepper.

SWEET RED ONION SAUCE

1. Pour a few swirls of oil into a skillet and add the chopped onions and garlic. Cook over medium-low heat for 15 to 20 minutes, stirring frequently, or until golden brown and softened, being careful not to burn the garlic.

2. Pour in the wine to deglaze the skillet, scraping up any browned bits from the bottom. Simmer for about 3 minutes until the wine evaporates.

3. Stir in the soffrito. Turn the heat to low and cook for about 10 minutes more, or until the vegetables are very soft.

4. Taste and season with salt and pepper.

Yield: 4 servings

Olive oil

1 pound (454 g) sweet red onions, peeled and finely chopped

1 garlic clove, peeled and finely chopped

½ cup (120 ml) white wine

¼ cup (33 g) Soffrito (page 11)

Salt and fresh-cracked black pepper

BEST ON:
- Cooked meats and fish (hot)
- Lasagna and cannelloni
- Pizza, focaccia, piadina

GOES WELL ON:
- Boiled potatoes
- Bruschetta and crostini
- Cooked pasta (any type)
- Cooked vegetables
- Eggs
- Gnocchi
- Rice and risotto
- Veloutés and cream soups

CHICKPEA SAUCE

Yield: 6 to 8 servings

Olive oil

2 potatoes, diced

2 garlic cloves, peeled and diced

1 onion, diced

1 celery stalk, diced

1 carrot, diced

2 pork ribs, deboned and diced

2 cups (480 g) cooked or
    canned chickpeas, chopped

¼ cup (60 ml) white wine

4 ounces (115 g) Tuscan kale
    (cavolo nero), chopped
    with ribs removed

1 bunch fresh parsley, chopped

3 fresh sage leaves, chopped

1 rosemary sprig, stemmed
    and chopped

Salt and fresh-cracked
    black pepper

1. Pour a few swirls of oil into a large skillet and add the potatoes, garlic, onion, celery, and carrot. Sauté over medium heat for about 5 minutes until softened and beginning to brown.

2. Add the pork and chickpeas and sauté for 5 minutes.

3. Pour in the wine to deglaze the skillet, scraping up any browned bits from the bottom. Turn the heat to low and add the kale, parsley, sage, and rosemary. Cook very slowly for about 20 minutes until the vegetables are soft and the sauce thickens, adding hot water if the sauce becomes dry.

4. Taste and season with salt and pepper.

BEST ON:
- Cooked pasta (any type)
- Pizza, focaccia, piadina

GOES WELL ON:
- Bruschetta and crostini
- Cooked vegetables
- Crespelle
- Stewed legumes
- Stuffed pasta (cheese, meat, seafood, or vegetables)

DUXELLES SAUCE

Yield: 4 to 6 servings

Olive oil

3½ tablespoons (49 g) butter

1 white onion, diced

1 pound (454 g) champignon
(white button) mushrooms,
finely chopped

¼ cup (33 g) Soffrito (page 11)

Salt and fresh-cracked
black pepper

1 bunch fresh parsley, chopped

BEST ON:
- Cooked meats and fish
  (hot or cold)
- Cooked pasta (all types)
- Pizza, focaccia, piadina
- Veloutés and cream soups

GOES WELL ON:
- Bruschetta and crostini
- Crespelle
- Gnocchi
- Lasagna and cannelloni
- Raw meats and fish:
  tartare and carpaccio
- Stewed legumes
- Stuffed pasta (cheese,
  meat, seafood, or vegetables)

1. In a skillet, combine the butter and a few swirls of oil. Add
   the onion and cook over low heat for 7 to 8 minutes, stirring
   occasionally, until translucent.

2. Add the mushrooms and soffrito. Turn the heat to high and
   cook for 5 minutes, stirring continuously with a wooden spoon,
   until the mushrooms release their liquid and soften.

3. Taste and season with salt and pepper, then sprinkle with plenty
   of chopped parsley.

CANNELLINI BEAN SAUCE

1. Place the beans in a food processor or blender, or into a medium-size bowl and use an immersion blender, and add the garlic. Blend the beans, adding water as needed to adjust the consistency, and drizzle in oil, until the sauce is thick and creamy.

2. Taste and season with salt and pepper and a pinch of cumin, then sprinkle on plenty of chopped parsley.

Yield: 4 servings

2 cups (364 g) cooked cannellini beans or canned, rinsed, and drained

2 garlic cloves, peeled and finely chopped

3 tablespoons (45 ml) water, plus more as needed

Olive oil

Salt and fresh-cracked black pepper

Ground cumin for seasoning

1 bunch fresh parsley, chopped

BEST ON:
- Grilled meat
- Roasted vegetables

GOES WELL ON:
- Bruschetta and crostini
- Cooked meats and fish (cold)
- Cooked pasta (all types)
- Raw meats and fish: tartare and carpaccio
- Stuffed pasta (cheese, meat, seafood, or vegetables)
- Veloutés and cream soups

SAUCE OF BEANS, MARROW, AND RED ONION

Yield: 6 to 8 servings

2 cups (364 g) cooked
cannellini beans or
canned, rinsed, and
drained

2 garlic cloves, peeled and
finely chopped

3½ tablespoons (52.5 g)
marrow

3 red onions, chopped

Salt and fresh-cracked
black pepper

BEST ON:
- Bruschetta and crostini
- Cooked pasta (any type)
- Grilled meats (hot)
- Pizza, focaccia, piadina

GOES WELL ON:
- Eggs
- Gnocchi
- Lasagna and cannelloni
- Rice and risotto
- Stuffed pasta (meat)
- Veloutés and cream soups

1. Place the beans in a food processor or blender, or a medium-size bowl and use an immersion blender, and add the garlic.

2. In a skillet over medium heat, melt the marrow. Add the onions and sauté for about 5 minutes, or until they soften and begin to brown, then add to the beans and blend until smooth.

3. Taste and season with salt and pepper.

BROAD BEAN SAUCE WITH PRIMO SALE CHEESE

1. Place the beans in a food processor or blender, or in a medium-size bowl and use an immersion blender, and blend until creamy, slowly adding oil, as needed. Transfer to a medium-size bowl. Taste and season with salt and pepper.

2. Clean the food processor or blender, or the bowl and immersion blender, and combine the primo sale cheese and milk in it. Blend until smooth. Taste and season with salt, pepper, paprika, and oil as needed.

3. Transfer the cheese sauce to the bowl with the bean purée and gently fold the two sauces into each other to combine, without too much mixing, so you have a variegated mixture.

Yield: 6 to 8 servings

1 cup (170 g) shelled fresh baby broad (fava) beans

Olive oil

Salt and fresh-cracked black pepper

¾ cup (90 g) primo sale cheese

¼ cup (60 ml) milk

1 pinch smoked paprika

BEST ON:
- Bruschetta and crostini
- Pasta salad

GOES WELL ON:
- Al dente pasta
- Boiled potatoes
- Cooked meats and fish (hot or cold)
- Crustaceans
- Gnocchi
- Pizza, focaccia, piadina
- Raw meats and fish: tartare and carpaccio

ZUCCHINI BLOSSOM SAUCE

Yield: 4 servings

1½ tablespoons (21 g) butter

1 shallot, peeled and chopped

About 10 ounces (280 g) zucchini blossoms, coarsely chopped

½ cup (120 ml) heavy cream

Salt and fresh-cracked black pepper

BEST ON:
- Bruschetta and crostini
- Cooked pasta (any type)

GOES WELL ON:
- Cook meat and fish (hot or cold)
- Cooked vegetables
- Gnocchi
- Lasagna and cannelloni
- Pizza, focaccia, piadina
- Stuffed pasta (cheese, meat, seafood, or vegetables)

I. In a skillet over medium heat, melt the butter. Add the shallot and sauté for 3 to 4 minutes, stirring occasionally, until the shallot begins to brown.

2. Add the zucchini blossoms, turn the heat to low, and cook for 2 minutes. Transfer the mixture to a food processor or blender, or use an immersion blender, and blend until smooth.

3. Return the sauce to the pan over low heat and pour in the cream. Simmer for about 5 minutes to heat through and thicken.

4. Taste and season with salt and pepper.

PORCINI MUSHROOM SAUCE

1. In a skillet over low heat, melt the butter. Add the shallot and cook for 5 to 10 minutes, stirring occasionally, until softened and beginning to brown.

2. Add the mushrooms in a single layer and cook for 10 minutes, stirring occasionally. Transfer the mushrooms and shallot to a food processor or blender, or use an immersion blender, pour in the cream, and blend until smooth. Return the sauce to the pan and simmer over low heat for 10 minutes to thicken the sauce.

3. Sprinkle the chopped parsley over the sauce.

4. Taste and season with salt and pepper.

Yield: 4 servings

1½ tablespoons (21 g) butter

1 shallot, peeled and chopped

1 pound (454 g) fresh porcini mushrooms, chopped

¾ cup (180 ml) heavy cream

1 bunch fresh parsley, chopped

Salt and fresh-cracked black pepper

BEST ON:
- Al dente pasta (all types)
- Rice and risotto

GOES WELL ON:
- Boiled potatoes
- Cooked meats and fish (hot or cold)
- Cooked vegetables
- Crespelle
- Crustaceans
- Gnocchi
- Polenta
- Stuffed pasta (cheese, meat, seafood, or vegetables)

OVOLI MUSHROOM SAUCE

Yield: 4 to 6 servings

1 pound (454 g) ovoli
  mushrooms, not fully
  opened, chopped with
  outer film removed

1 bunch fresh parsley,
  chopped

¼ cup (60 ml) light olive oil

2 tablespoons (30 ml) freshly
  squeezed lemon juice

Salt and fresh-cracked
  black pepper

BEST ON:
- Al dente pasta
- Pasta salad

GOES WELL ON:
- Boiled potatoes
- Cooked meats and fish
  (hot or cold)
- Crustaceans
- Eggs
- Gnocchi
- Raw meats and fish:
  tartare and carpaccio
- Rice and risotto
- Veloutés and cream soups

1. Place the mushrooms and parsley into a large bowl.

2. In a small bowl, whisk the oil, lemon juice, and a pinch of salt and pepper until emulsified. Pour the dressing over the mushrooms and toss to coat and combine.

SAUCE OF OVOLI MUSHROOMS, CELERY, AND GRUYÈRE

1. Place the celery, Gruyère, mushrooms, and parsley in a large bowl.

2. In a small bowl, whisk the oil, lemon juice, and a pinch of salt and pepper until emulsified. Pour the dressing over the vegetables and toss to coat and combine.

Yield: 4 to 6 servings

4 ounces (115 g) celery, diced

4 ounces (115 g) Gruyère cheese, diced

1 pound (454 g) ovoli mushrooms, not fully opened, chopped with film removed

1 bunch fresh parsley, chopped

¼ cup (60 ml) light olive oil

2 tablespoons (30 ml) freshly squeezed lemon juice

Salt and fresh-cracked black pepper

BEST ON:
- Pasta salad

GOES WELL ON:
- Al dente pasta
- Boiled potatoes
- Cooked meats and fish (hot or cold)
- Crustaceans
- Eggs
- Gnocchi
- Raw meats and fish: tartare and carpaccio
- Rice and risotto
- Veloutés and cream soups

THE WHOLE GARDEN SAUCE

Yield: 4 to 6 servings

1 pound (454 g) cherry
  tomatoes, coarsely chopped

2 leeks, trimmed and coarsely
  chopped

8 ounces (225 g) carrots

2 red onions, chopped

2 shallots, chopped

2 celery stalks, chopped

2 zucchini, chopped

1 red bell pepper, chopped

1 yellow bell pepper, chopped

¼ cup (33 g) Soffrito (page 11)

Olive oil

1 bunch fresh basil

Salt and fresh-cracked
  black pepper

1. Place the tomatoes, leeks, carrots, onions, shallots, celery, zucchini, and red and yellow bell peppers in a saucepan.

2. Stir in the soffrito and pour in a few generous swirls of oil. Place the pan over medium heat, and cook for 30 minutes, stirring occasionally, until the vegetables soften and meld together in a thick sauce.

3. Tear the basil leaves into pieces and stir them into the sauce.

4. Taste and season with salt and pepper.

BEST ON:
- Cooked pasta (all types)
- Lasagna and cannelloni
- Stuffed pasta (cheese, meat, seafood, or vegetables)

GOES WELL ON:
- Bruschetta and crostini

- Cooked meats and fish (hot or cold)
- Crespelle
- Gnocchi
- Pasta salad
- Pizza, focaccia, piadina
- Raw meats and fish: tartare and carpaccio

GENOVESE SAUCE

Yield: 6 to 8 servings

1 soft dinner roll

Red wine vinegar for
seasoning

1½ tablespoons (14 g) pine nuts

3 tablespoons (27 g) brined
capers, drained

12 pitted black olives

1 bunch fresh parsley

1 garlic clove, peeled

1 egg yolk

6 tablespoons (90 ml) olive oil

¼ cup (60 ml) freshly squeezed
lemon juice, strained

Salt and fresh-cracked
black pepper

1. Tear the roll into pieces, place them into a small bowl, and add a few good splashes of vinegar. Let soak while you toast the pine nuts.

2. Meanwhile, in a small nonstick skillet over medium-high heat, toast the pine nuts for 2 to 3 minutes until lightly browned and fragrant. Let cool slightly, then transfer to a blender.

3. Add the capers, olives, parsley, and garlic clove to the blender. Squeeze the roll to remove as much vinegar as possible and add the soaked bread pieces to the blender, along with egg yolk. While blending, slowly pour in the oil, a little at a time, then the lemon juice and blend until smooth and creamy.

4. Taste and season with salt and pepper.

BEST ON:
- Pasta salad
- Rice salad

GOES WELL ON:
- Al dente pasta
- Boiled potatoes
- Bruschetta and crostini
- Cooked meats and fish
  (hot or cold)
- Cooked vegetables
- Gnocchi
- Pizza, focaccia, piadina
- Veloutés and cream soups

ALL-PURPOSE LENTIL SAUCE

1. Rinse the lentils well and put them in a large pot. Pour in enough vegetable broth to cover, add the bay leaves, and bring to a simmer over low heat. Once at a simmer, cook for 10 minutes.

2. Drain the lentils, reserving the cooking water, and discard the bay leaves.

3. Put the lentils in a food processor or blender, add the yogurt, season with your spices of choice to taste, pour in the oil, and add a pinch of salt. Blend on high speed, adding some of the reserved cooking water as needed, until creamy. If you prefer it even creamier, pass the sauce through a fine-mesh sieve set over a bowl. Serve hot or at room temperature.

Yield: 8 to 10 servings

1 pound (454 g) dried lentils

Vegetable broth
    for cooking

2 bay leaves

1 cup (230 g) yogurt

Spices for seasoning
    (such as dried basil,
    oregano, rosemary,
    thyme, red pepper flakes)

¼ cup (60 ml) vegetable oil

Salt

BEST ON:
- Cooked pasta (all types)
- Rice and risotto

GOES WELL ON:
- Cooked meats or fish
  (hot or cold)
- Crespelle
- Crustaceans
- Eggs

- Gnocchi
- Lasagna and cannelloni
- Pasta salad
- Pizza, focaccia, piadina
- Polenta
- Raw meats and fish:
  tartare and carpaccio
- Stuffed pasta (cheese,
  meat, seafood, or vegetables)
- Veloutés and cream soups

CREAMY LENTIL SAUCE

Yield: 4 to 6 servings

1½ tablespoons (21 g) butter

1 shallot, peeled and chopped

1½ cups (288 g) dried lentils

4½ cups (1 L) water

½ cup (120 ml) heavy cream

Salt and fresh-cracked
    black pepper

BEST ON:
- Bruschetta and crostini
- Cooked pasta (all types)
- Pizza, focaccia, piadina

GOES WELL ON:
- Cooked meats and fish
  (hot or cold)
- Cooked vegetables
- Crespelle
- Crustaceans
- Raw meats and fish:
  tartare and carpaccio
- Stuffed pasta (cheese,
  meat, seafood, or vegetables)

1. In a saucepan over medium heat, melt the butter. Add the shallot and cook for about 3 minutes, stirring occasionally, until the shallot begins to soften and brown.

2. As soon as the shallot takes on some color, rinse the lentils well and add them to the pan, along with the water. Bring to a boil, reduce the heat to maintain a simmer, cover the pan, and cook for 15 to 20 minutes until the lentils are soft and most of the water is absorbed. Transfer to a food processor or blender, or use an immersion blender, and blend until smooth. Return the lentils to the pot and place it over medium heat.

3. Stir in the cream and simmer for 3 to 5 minutes to thicken the sauce.

4. Taste and season with salt and pepper.

EGGPLANT CAPONATA

Yield: 6 to 8 servings

1. In a medium-size bowl, combine the raisins with enough hot water to cover and let soak for 20 minutes. Drain and squeeze the excess water from the raisins.

2. Pour a few swirls of olive oil into a large skillet and add the sliced vegetables. Sauté over medium heat for about 10 minutes until softened and browned.

3. Stir in the tomato purée and cook for 15 minutes. Transfer the vegetable mixture to a food processor or blender, or use an immersion blender, and blend until smooth. Return the sauce to the skillet.

4. In another skillet, heat a few tablespoons (45 ml) of sunflower seed oil over medium-high heat until shimmering. Add the eggplant and sauté for 3 to 4 minutes until golden brown. Using a slotted spoon, transfer the eggplant to paper towel to drain, then add it to the tomato sauce.

5. Stir in the olives, soaked raisins, capers, and vinegar and cook for 20 minutes, stirring occasionally until slightly thickened and hot.

6. Taste and season with sugar, salt, and pepper.

1 handful raisins

2 white onions, sliced

2 carrots, sliced

1 celery stalk, sliced

1 red bell pepper, sliced

Olive oil

2 cups (500 g) tomato purée

Sunflower seed oil

2 pounds (908 g) eggplant, cubed

½ cup (50 g) mixed pitted olives

2 tablespoons (18 g) brined capers, drained

¼ cup (60 ml) white wine vinegar

Sugar for seasoning

Salt and fresh-cracked black pepper

BEST ON:
- Bruschetta and crostini
- Cooked pasta (all types)

GOES WELL ON:
- Cooked meats and fish (hot or cold)
- Crespelle
- Eggs
- Gnocchi
- Pasta salad

- Pizza, focaccia, piadina
- Polenta
- Raw meats and fish: tartare and carpaccio
- Rice and risotto
- Veloutés and cream soups

EGGPLANT AND BELL PEPPER SAUCE

Yield: 6 to 8 servings

4 eggplants

10 bell peppers, any color

Olive oil

1 onion, chopped

2 garlic cloves, peeled
and chopped

1 bunch fresh parsley,
chopped

1 tablespoon freshly squeezed
lemon juice, strained

Salt and fresh-cracked
black pepper

BEST ON:
- Cooked meats (hot)
- Cooked pasta (all types)

GOES WELL ON:
- Boiled potatoes
- Crespelle
- Crustaceans
- Gnocchi
- Lasagna and cannelloni
- Pasta salad
- Polenta
- Stewed legumes
- Stuffed pasta (cheese,
  meat, seafood, or vegetables)

1. Preheat the oven to 350°F (180°C, or gas mark 4).

2. Place the eggplants and bell peppers on a large sheet pan (or two pans) and bake for 30 minutes, or until soft. Let cool until the vegetables can be handled, then remove the skins, stems, and seeds from the peppers. Halve the eggplants and remove the pulp and seeds.

3. Scoop the roasted eggplant flesh from each half into a food processor or blender and add the peppers. Blend until smooth.

4. Pour in a few swirls of oil into a saucepan and add the onion. Cook over medium heat for about 10 minutes, stirring occasionally, until translucent. Add the garlic and sauté for about 30 seconds until fragrant.

5. Add the eggplant and pepper purée to the pan, along with ¼ cup (60 ml) of oil, and whisk until emulsified.

6. Add the parsley to the sauce, along with the lemon juice. Whisk to combine.

7. Taste and season with salt and pepper.

EGGPLANT, OLIVE, AND CAPER SAUCE

Yield: 6 to 8 servings

1. In a large skillet, heat a few tablespoons (45 ml) of sunflower seed oil over medium-high heat until shimmering. Add the eggplant and sauté for 3 to 4 minutes until golden brown. Using a slotted spoon, transfer the eggplant to paper towel to drain.

2. Wipe out the skillet and place it over medium heat. Pour in a few swirls of olive oil and add the celery and onions. Sauté for about 3 minutes until the vegetables begin to soften.

3. Stir in the soffrito, olives, capers, and eggplant.

4. Pour in the wine to deglaze the skillet, scraping up any browned bits from the bottom. Simmer for about 3 minutes until the wine evaporates.

5. Taste and season with salt and pepper.

Sunflower seed oil

2 pounds (908 g) eggplant, diced

Olive oil

1 celery stalk, sliced

2 white onions, thinly sliced

¼ cup (33 g) Soffrito (page 11)

½ cup (50 g) pitted green olives, coarsely chopped

2 tablespoons (18 g) salt-packed capers, rinsed

½ cup (120 ml) dry white wine

Salt and fresh-cracked black pepper

BEST ON:
- Bruschetta and crostini
- Cooked pasta (all types)

GOES WELL ON:
- Cooked meats and fish (hot or cold)
- Cooked vegetables
- Crustaceans

- Gnocchi
- Lasagna and cannelloni
- Pasta salad
- Raw meats and fish: tartare and carpaccio
- Rice and risotto
- Stewed legumes
- Stuffed pasta (cheese, meat, seafood, or vegetables)

YELLOW MILANESE SAUCE

Yield: 4 to 6 servings

7 tablespoons (98 g) butter

1 white onion, thinly sliced

3½ tablespoons (25 g)
    potato starch

¼ cup (60 ml) dry white wine

1 medium pinch (about
    35 threads) saffron threads

1 cup (20 ml) broth of choice,
    heated

2 tablespoons (16 g) Soffrito
    (page 11)

Salt and fresh-cracked
    black pepper

BEST ON:
- Cooked pasta (all types)
- Rice and risotto

GOES WELL ON:
- Boiled potatoes
- Cooked vegetables
- Crustaceans
- Gnocchi
- Stuffed pasta (cheese,
    meat, seafood, or vegetables)

1. In a saucepan over low heat, melt the butter. Add the onion and cook over low heat for about 10 minutes, stirring occasionally, to sweat the onion until it is soft and translucent.

2. Stirring vigorously with a wooden spoon, sprinkle in the potato starch and pour in the wine, stirring until combined.

3. In a small bowl, dissolve the saffron threads in the hot broth and add it to the pan. Cook, stirring constantly so no lumps form, until the sauce thickens.

4. Stir in the soffrito.

5. Taste and season with salt and pepper.

SAUCE ALLA NORMA

1. Add the garlic to a saucepan with a few swirls of olive oil. Sauté over medium heat for about 30 seconds until fragrant.

2. Add the basil to the pan, along with the tomatoes. Season with salt and pepper to taste, stir to combine, and cook for 10 minutes, stirring occasionally to help break up the tomatoes.

3. In a skillet over medium-high heat, heat a few tablespoons (45 ml) of sesame seed oil until shimmering. Add the eggplant and sauté for 3 to 4 minutes until golden brown. Using a slotted spoon, transfer the eggplant to paper towel to drain, then add the eggplant to the saucepan.

4. Stir in the soffrito and cook for 10 minutes, stirring occasionally, until the sauce is thickened and heated through.

5. Taste and season with salt and pepper.

Yield: 4 servings

1 garlic clove, peeled and finely chopped

Olive oil

1 bunch fresh basil, chopped

8 ounces (225 g) peeled tomatoes (canned is fine)

Salt and fresh-cracked black pepper

Sesame seed oil

1 pound (454 g) eggplant, cubed

2 tablespoons (16 g) Soffrito (page 11)

BEST ON:
- Cooked pasta (all types)
- Crespelle

GOES WELL ON:
- Bruschetta and crostini
- Cooked meats (hot)
- Crustaceans
- Eggs
- Gnocchi
- Pizza, focaccia, piadina
- Polenta
- Rice and risotto
- Veloutés and cream soups

WALNUT SAUCE

Yield: 4 servings

2 slices dry white bread

Milk

1 pound (454 g) shelled walnuts

2 fresh myrtle leaves or bay leaves

1 garlic clove, peeled

4 ounces (115 g) ricotta (preferably sheep's milk)

⅔ cup (160 ml) extra-virgin olive oil (preferably Ligurian)

Salt and fresh-cracked black pepper

1. Tear the bread into pieces and place them in a medium bowl. Pour in enough milk to cover and let soak while you prepare the walnuts. Drain and squeeze the excess milk from the bread.

2. Bring a large pot of water to a boil. Break up the walnuts, throw the pieces into the boiling water, and cook for 1 minute. Drain, let cool, and remove the skins, if needed.

3. Transfer the walnuts to a food processor or blender and add the soaked bread, myrtle leaves, garlic, ricotta, and oil. Blend well.

4. Taste and season with salt and pepper.

BEST ON:
- Cooked pasta (all types, especially egg pasta)

GOES WELL ON:
- Bruschetta and crostini
- Cooked meats and fish (hot or cold)
- Crespelle
- Gnocchi
- Pasta salad
- Pizza, focaccia, piadina
- Polenta
- Raw meats and fish: tartare and carpaccio
- Rice salad
- Veloutés and cream soups

HAZELNUT SAUCE

Yield: 4 servings

1 cup (135 g) hazelnuts

1 garlic clove, peeled

⅔ cup (160 ml) extra-virgin
   olive oil

4 ounces (115 g) grated
   Pecorino Romano cheese

Salt and fresh-cracked
   black pepper

BEST ON:
- Cooked pasta (all types)

GOES WELL ON:
- Bruschetta and crostini
- Cooked meats and fish
  (hot or cold)
- Cooked vegetables
- Crespelle
- Pasta salad
- Raw meats and fish:
  tartare and carpaccio
- Rice salad

1. In a food processor, combine the hazelnuts and garlic. Turn the processor on and slowly pour in the oil, blending until you have a smooth sauce.

2. Add the cheese and pulse to combine. If the sauce is for a pasta, add the cheese after dressing the pasta with the sauce.

3. Taste and season with salt and pepper.

MOUNTAIN POTATO SAUCE

1. Bring a large pot of water to a boil. Add the whole unpeeled potatoes and cook until soft. Drain, let cool slightly, peel, and mash the potatoes. Transfer the potatoes to a heavy-bottomed saucepan and add the milk and a pinch of nutmeg. Stir and bring to a boil.

2. Transfer the potato mixture to a food processor, or use an immersion blender. While blending, trickle in the oil until the consistency is smooth and uniform. Continue blending (it may take a while)—the texture will begin to change, becoming frothier and lighter.

3. Taste and season with salt and pepper.

Yield: 4 servings

1 pound (454 g) mountain, russet, or Yukon Gold potatoes

2 cups (480 ml) whole milk

Freshly grated nutmeg for seasoning

Olive oil

Salt and fresh-cracked black pepper

BEST ON:
- Cooked meats and fish (hot or cold)

GOES WELL ON:
- Cooked pasta (all types)
- Crustaceans
- Veloutés and cream soups

CHAMPAGNE POTATO SAUCE

Yield: 4 servings

Olive oil

About 10 ounces (280 g) russet potatoes, peeled and sliced

1 bunch wild garlic blossoms or fresh garlic chives, chopped

½ cup (120 ml) Champagne or other sparkling white wine

1 fresh chile pepper (such as serrano or jalapeño), destemmed, seeded and minced

1 cup (240 ml) water

Salt and fresh-cracked black pepper

3½ tablespoons (53 g) mascarpone cheese

3 tablespoons (45 ml) heavy cream

BEST ON:
• Hot fish fillets

GOES WELL ON:
• Cooked meats (hot or cold)
• Cooked pasta
• Veloutés and cream soups

1. Pour a few swirls of oil into a large skillet, arrange the potato slices in a single layer, and sprinkle with the chopped blossoms. Cook over medium heat for about 7 minutes, or until the potatoes begin to brown.

2. Pour in the Champagne to deglaze the skillet, scraping up any browned bits from the bottom.

3. Add the chile and water. Bring to a simmer and cook until the potatoes are tender and most of the liquid has evaporated. Transfer the potatoes to a food processor or blender, or use an immersion blender. Let cool slightly. Season with salt and pepper.

4. Add the mascarpone cheese and cream. While blending, drizzle in the oil a little at a time until you have a purée.

5. Taste again and reseason as needed.

RED BELL PEPPER SAUCE

1. If using fresh peppers, preheat the broiler, or a grill to high heat.

2. Broil or grill the fresh bell peppers until their skins are blackened all over, turning frequently. Transfer to a large bowl and cover with plastic wrap, or to a paper bag and seal the bag. Let steam for about 15 minutes, or until cool enough to handle. Peel off the skins and remove the stems and seeds.

3. Pour a few swirls of oil into a saucepan and add the onion and garlic clove. Sauté over medium heat for 3 to 5 minutes until softened and beginning to brown. Transfer the onion and garlic to a food processor or blender, leaving the oil in the pan.

4. Add the tomatoes, roasted bell peppers, soffrito, chile, and water to the sauce and bring to a simmer over medium heat. Cook until the vegetables are soft. Transfer the sauce to the food processor or blender with the onion and garlic, or use an immersion blender, and blend until smooth.

5. Taste and season with salt and pepper.

Yield: 4 to 6 servings

4 red bell peppers or 4 jarred roasted red peppers, rinsed

Olive oil

1 white onion, diced

1 garlic clove, peeled

3 large tomatoes, diced

¼ cup (33 g) Soffrito (page 11)

1 fresh chile pepper (such as serrano or jalapeño), destemmed, seeded and chopped

¼ cup (60 ml) water, or more as needed

Salt and fresh-cracked black pepper

BEST ON:
- Cooked pasta (all types)
- Stuffed pasta (cheese, meat, seafood, or vegetables)

GOES WELL ON:
- Bruschetta and crostini
- Cooked meats or fish (hot or cold)
- Cooked vegetables
- Crespelle
- Crustaceans
- Eggs
- Gnocchi
- Pasta salad
- Raw meats and fish: tartare and carpaccio

ROSEMARY POTATO SAUCE

Yield: 4 to 6 servings

3½ tablespoons (49 g) butter

1 small white onion, finely diced

1 pound (454 g) potatoes, peeled and coarsely chopped

1 rosemary sprig, stemmed and finely chopped

¼ cup (30 g) all-purpose flour

1½ cups (360 ml) heavy cream

Salt and fresh-cracked black pepper

BEST ON:
- Roast beef

GOES WELL ON:
- Cooked meats and fish (hot or cold)
- Crustaceans
- Veloutés and cream soups

1. In a large saucepan over medium heat, melt the butter. Add the onion and sauté for about 4 minutes until it begins to soften.

2. Add the potatoes and rosemary, sprinkle with flour, pour in enough water to cover, and cook until the potatoes are tender.

3. Transfer the mixture to a food processor or blender, or use an immersion blender, and blend until smooth. Return the potatoes to the saucepan and place over low heat.

4. Stir in the cream and cook for about 10 minutes to thicken the sauce.

5. Taste and season with salt and pepper.

YELLOW BELL PEPPER SAUCE WITH TURMERIC

Yield: 4 servings

4 yellow bell peppers

Olive oil

1 white onion, diced

1 fresh chile pepper (such as serrano or jalapeño), destemmed, seeded and chopped

1 garlic clove, unpeeled

¼ cup (33 g) Soffrito (page 11)

¼ cup (60 ml) water, or more as needed

1 teaspoon ground turmeric

Salt and fresh-cracked black pepper

1. Preheat the broiler, or a grill to high heat.

2. Broil or grill the bell peppers until their skins are blackened all over, turning frequently. Transfer to a large bowl and cover with plastic wrap, or to a paper bag and seal the bag. Let steam for about 15 minutes, or until cool enough to handle. Peel off the skins and remove the stems and seeds. Roughly chop the bell peppers.

3. Pour a few swirls of oil into a saucepan and add the onion, chile, and garlic clove. Sauté over medium heat for 3 to 5 minutes until the vegetables soften and begin to brown. Crush the garlic with a wooden spoon, stir it into the oil to flavor it, then remove and discard the garlic.

4. Add the bell peppers, soffrito, and water to the saucepan and bring to a simmer. Cook until the vegetables are soft. Transfer the sauce to the food processor or blender, or use an immersion blender, add the turmeric, and blend until smooth.

5. Taste and season with salt and pepper.

BEST ON:
- Cooked pasta (all types)
- Grilled crustaceans
- Stuffed pasta (cheese, meat, seafood, or vegetables)

GOES WELL ON:
- Bruschetta and crostini

- Cooked meats or fish (hot or cold)
- Cooked vegetables
- Crespelle
- Eggs
- Gnocchi
- Pasta salad
- Raw meats and fish: tartare and carpaccio

MILD GREEN CHILE SAUCE

1. In a food processor or blender, or in a medium-size bowl using an immersion blender, combine the chiles, onion, garlic, lemon juice, chili powder to taste, and soffrito. While blending, slowly trickle in the oil until the mixture is homogeneous, but not too smooth.

2. Taste and season with salt and pepper. Refrigerate until ready to serve, either cold or at room temperature.

Yield: 4 to 6 servings

1 pound (454 g) sweet green chile peppers (such as Anaheim, Cubanelle, Frontera, or poblano), roughly chopped

1 white onion, chopped

1 garlic clove, chopped

Juice of 1 lemon

Chili powder for seasoning

2 tablespoons (16 g) Soffrito (page 11)

Olive oil

Salt and fresh-cracked black pepper

BEST ON:
- Grilled meats and fish
- Pasta salad
- Raw meats and fish: tartare and carpaccio

GOES WELL ON:
- Bruschetta and crostini
- Cooked pasta (all types)
- Crespelle
- Eggs
- Pasta salad
- Rice salad
- Veloutés and cream soups

BELL PEPPER, TOMATO, AND EGGPLANT SAUCE

Yield: 6 to 8 servings

4 red bell peppers or 4 jarred
  roasted red peppers, rinsed

About 10 ounces (280 g)
  purple eggplant

Olive oil

1 white onion, chopped

1 garlic clove, unpeeled

3 large tomatoes, diced

1 fresh chile pepper (such
  as serrano or jalapeño),
  destemmed, seeded
  and chopped

2 tablespoons (30 ml) freshly
  squeezed lemon juice

Salt and fresh-cracked
  black pepper

BEST ON:
- Cooked pasta (all types)
- Pasta salad
- Stuffed pasta (cheese, meat,
  seafood, or vegetables)

GOES WELL ON:
- Bruschetta and crostini
- Cooked meats and fish
  (hot or cold)
- Eggs
- Gnocchi

1. If using fresh pepper, preheat the broiler, or a grill to high heat.

2. Broil or grill the fresh bell peppers until their skins are blackened all over, turning frequently. Transfer to a large bowl and cover with plastic wrap, or to a paper bag and seal the bag. Let steam for about 15 minutes, or until cool enough to handle. Peel off the skins and remove the stems and seeds. Roughly chop the bell peppers.

3. While the peppers steam, preheat the oven to 350°F (180°C, or gas mark 4), or a grill to medium heat.

4. Place the eggplant on a sheet pan and bake for 30 minutes, or until soft. Let cool slightly, then roughly chop the eggplant. There is no need to peel it.

5. Pour a few swirls of oil into a saucepan and add the onion and unpeeled garlic clove. Sauté over medium heat for about 3 minutes until softened and beginning to brown. Crush the garlic with a wooden spoon, stir it into the oil to flavor it, then remove and discard the garlic.

6. Add the tomatoes, roasted bell peppers and eggplant, and the chile. Cook for about 10 minutes to soften the vegetables, adding hot water as needed if the sauce becomes dry. Transfer the sauce to a food processor or blender, or use an immersion blender, add the lemon juice, and blend until smooth.

7. Taste and season with salt and pepper.

PEA SAUCE WITH FRESH MINT

Yield: 4 to 6 servings

1 pound (454 g) shelled peas, fresh or frozen and thawed

1 garlic clove, peeled

1 bunch fresh mint

1¼ cups (290 g) yogurt

Salt and fresh-cracked black pepper

Olive oil

BEST ON:
- Pasta salad
- Cooked vegetables (served cold or at room temperature)

GOES WELL ON:
- Bruschetta and crostini
- Cooked meats and fish (cold)
- Eggs
- Raw meats and fish: tartare and carpaccio
- Rice salad

1. Bring a saucepan full of water to a boil. Add the peas and blanch for 1 minute. Drain and rinse with cool water to stop the cooking. Drain again.

2. Transfer the peas to a food processor or blender, or to a medium-size bowl and use immersion blender. Add the garlic, mint, and yogurt. Blend until smooth.

3. Taste and season with salt and pepper, then finish with a drizzle of oil. Blend again to combine. Serve cold or at room temperature.

PEA AND RICOTTA SAUCE

1. In a small nonstick skillet over medium-high heat, toast the walnuts for 2 to 3 minutes until lightly browned and fragrant. Let cool.

2. Bring a saucepan full of water to a boil. Add the peas and blanch for 1 minute. Drain and rinse with cool water to stop the cooking. Drain again.

3. Pour half of the peas into a food processor or blender, or into a medium-size bowl and use an immersion blender, and blend, adding a little oil at a time, until you have a smooth sauce.

4. Place the ricotta in a medium-size bowl and pour in the pea purée. Add the remaining cooked peas, garlic, and walnuts and stir to combine.

5. Taste and season with salt and pepper.

Yield: 4 servings

¼ cup (30 g) chopped walnuts

1 pound (454 g) shelled peas, fresh or frozen and thawed

Olive oil

¾ cup (195 g) ricotta (preferably sheep's milk)

1 garlic clove, peeled and minced

Salt and fresh-cracked black pepper

BEST ON:
- Al dente penne (or other ridged pasta)
- Bruschetta and crostini
- Pasta salad

GOES WELL ON:
- Boiled potatoes
- Cooked meats and fish (hot or cold)
- Crustaceans
- Gnocchi
- Raw meats and fish: tartare and carpaccio
- Rice and risotto
- Rice salad
- Stuffed pasta (cheese, meat, seafood, or vegetables)

ESCAROLE SAUCE

Yield: 6 to 8 servings

Olive oil

1 garlic clove, unpeeled

1 pound (454 g) escarole, finely sliced

1 pound spreadable cheese (such as fresh mozzarella, ricotta, or stracciatella)

1 bunch fresh mint

Salt and fresh-cracked black pepper

BEST ON:
- Bruschetta and crostini

GOES WELL ON:
- Cooked meats and fish (hot or cold)
- Cooked vegetables
- Gnocchi
- Pasta salad
- Stuffed pasta (cheese or vegetables)

1. Pour a swirl or two of oil into a skillet, add the unpeeled garlic clove, and sauté over medium heat for 2 to 3 minutes to soften and brown. Crush the garlic with a wooden spoon.

2. Add the escarole to the skillet. Turn the heat to high and sauté for about 5 minutes until wilted and soft, adding a little water if the skillet becomes dry. Remove from the heat and let cool. Remove and discard the garlic clove.

3. Transfer the escarole to a food processor or blender, or use an immersion blender. Add the cheese and mint and blend until smooth.

4. Taste and season with salt and pepper.

PEASANT'S SAUCE

1. Add the garlic to a saucepan, then pour in a few swirls of oil. Sauté over medium heat for about 30 seconds until fragrant.

2. Add the tomatoes, celery, capers, soffrito, and oregano. Tear the basil leaves with your hands and add them to the pan, stirring to combine. Sauté for 7 to 10 minutes, or until the vegetables soften, the tomatoes begin to break down, and the sauce thickens slightly.

3. Taste and season with salt and pepper.

1 garlic clove, peeled and chopped

Olive oil

About 5 ounces (140 g) cherry tomatoes, roughly chopped

1 celery stalk, roughly chopped

1 tablespoon (9 g) salt-packed capers, rinsed and minced

¼ cup (33 g) Soffrito (page 11)

1 teaspoon dried oregano

1 bunch fresh basil

Salt and fresh-cracked black pepper

BEST ON:
- Cooked pasta (all types)

GOES WELL ON:
- Boiled potatoes
- Bruschetta and crostini
- Cooked meats and fish (hot or cold)
- Crespelle
- Crustaceans
- Eggs
- Gnocchi
- Polenta
- Rice and risotto
- Stuffed pasta (cheese, meat, seafood, or vegetables)

RED RADICCHIO AND WALNUT SAUCE

Yield: 2 to 4 servings

1¾ cups (175 g) walnuts

Olive oil

1 pound (454 g) red
   radicchio, coarsely
   chopped

1 garlic clove, unpeeled

2 tablespoons (16 g)
   Soffrito (page 11)

Salt and fresh-cracked
   black pepper

BEST ON:
- Al dente penne (or other
  ridged pasta)
- Pasta salad

GOES WELL ON:
- Cooked meats and fish
  (cold)
- Crespelle
- Raw meats and fish:
  tartare and carpaccio
- Rice and risotto
- Rice salad

1. In a skillet over medium-high heat, toast the walnuts for 3 to
   5 minutes, stirring frequently, until lightly browned and fragrant.
   Transfer to a plate and set aside.

2. Pour a few swirls of oil into the skillet and add the radicchio and
   garlic clove. Sauté over high heat for 5 minutes, adding a bit of
   water if needed, until the radicchio wilts and softens, being careful
   not to burn the garlic. Remove and discard the garlic clove.

3. Transfer half of the radicchio to a food processor or blender and
   blend until smooth. Return the purée to the skillet, add the soffrito,
   and stir to combine.

4. Coarsely chop the walnuts and stir them into the sauce.

5. Taste and season with salt and pepper.

SPINACH SAUCE WITH CUMIN

Yield: 4 servings

2 pounds (908 g) fresh
    spinach

½ cup (120 ml) heavy cream

1 teaspoon ground cumin

Olive oil

2 garlic cloves, peeled
    and minced

Salt and fresh-cracked
    black pepper

BEST ON:
- Cooked pasta (all types)
- Lasagna and cannelloni

GOES WELL ON:
- Boiled potatoes
- Cooked meats and fish
    (hot or cold)
- Cooked vegetables
- Gnocchi
- Pasta salad
- Raw meats and fish:
    tartare and carpaccio
- Rice and risotto
- Stuffed pasta (cheese,
    meat, seafood, or vegetables)

1. Prepare an ice bath.

2. Bring a saucepan full of water to boil. Add the spinach and
   blanch for 2 minutes. Drain, transfer to the ice bath to stop
   the cooking, and drain again. Transfer the spinach to a food
   processor or blender.

3. Pour the cream into the food processor and add the cumin.
   Blend until smooth, adding just enough oil to form a purée.

4. Place the garlic in the now-empty saucepan with a swirl or
   two of oil. Sauté over medium heat for about 1 minute until
   it begins to soften and is fragrant.

5. Stir the spinach purée into the saucepan and simmer for a
   few minutes to heat through and thicken slightly.

6. Taste and season with salt and pepper.

SPINACH SAUCE WITH MOZZARELLA

1. Place the fresh mozzarella cubes in a colander and let drain for 30 minutes.

2. Meanwhile, prepare an ice bath.

3. Bring a saucepan full of water to boil. Add the spinach and blanch for 2 minutes. Drain, transfer to the ice bath to stop the cooking, and drain again. Transfer the spinach to a food processor or blender.

4. Pour the cream into the food processor and add the grana. Blend until smooth, adding just enough oil to form a purée.

5. Place the garlic in the now-empty saucepan with a swirl or two of oil. Sauté over medium heat for about 1 minute until it begins to soften and is fragrant.

6. Stir the spinach purée into the saucepan and simmer for a few minutes to heat through and thicken slightly.

7. Add the mozzarella to the sauce and cook for 30 seconds until heated through and the cheese begins to melt.

8. Taste and season with salt and pepper.

Yield: 4 to 6 servings

1 cup (150 g) cubed fresh mozzarella cheese

2 pounds (908 g) fresh spinach

½ cup (120 ml) heavy cream

1½ cups (150 g) grated grana (such as Asiago, Parmigiano-Reggiano, or Pecorino Romano)

2 garlic cloves, peeled and minced

Olive oil

Salt and fresh-cracked black pepper

BEST ON:
- Cooked pasta (all types)
- Lasagna and cannelloni

GOES WELL ON:
- Boiled potatoes
- Bruschetta and crostini
- Cooked meats and fish (hot or cold)
- Cooked pasta (all types)
- Eggs
- Gnocchi
- Raw meats and fish: tartare and carpaccio
- Rice and risotto
- Veloutés and cream soups

TORCELLANA SAUCE

Yield: 4 to 6 servings

Olive oil

1½ pounds (681 g) mixed
seasonal vegetables (such
as artichokes, asparagus,
bell peppers, eggplant,
mushrooms, onion, peas),
trimmed and diced

2 garlic cloves, peeled and
minced

About 10 ounces (280 g)
zucchini, peeled and diced

1 bunch fresh parsley, chopped

¼ cup (33 g) Soffrito (page 11)

½ cup (120 ml) vegetable broth

Salt and fresh-cracked
black pepper

1. Pour a few swirls of oil into a large skillet and sauté each vegetable
separately over medium heat, with a bit of the garlic, drizzling in
more oil as needed. Cook time will vary according to the vegetables
you use—keep them all very al dente.

2. Return the skillet to medium heat, pour in a drizzle of oil, and
add the zucchini. Sauté for 2 minutes until it starts to soften
and brown.

3. Return the sautéed seasonal vegetables to the skillet and stir
in the parsley and soffrito. Pour in the broth and cook for about
3 minutes to thicken the sauce.

4. Taste and season with salt and pepper.

BEST ON:
- Cooked pasta (all types)
- Rice and risotto

GOES WELL ON:
- Boiled potatoes
- Bruschetta and crostini
- Cooked meats and fish
  (hot or cold)

- Eggs
- Gnocchi
- Lasagna and cannelloni
- Pasta salad
- Pizza, focaccia, piadina
- Polenta
- Raw meats and fish:
  tartare and carpaccio
- Veloutés and cream soups

PUMPKIN PANCETTA SAUCE

1. Place the garlic in a skillet with a few swirls of oil. Sauté over medium heat for about 1 minute until fragrant and beginning to brown.

2. Add the pumpkin (if using pumpkin purée, add it in step 6), pour in enough broth to cover, turn the heat to low, and simmer for about 20 minutes, or until tender. Transfer the pumpkin mixture to a food processor or blender, or use an immersion blender, add the lemon juice, and blend until smooth.

3. Wipe out the skillet and return it to medium heat.

4. Add the pancetta to the skillet. Cook for about 5 minutes, stirring occasionally, until browned and crispy.

5. Stir in the puréed pumpkin, or canned pumpkin purée, and a splash or two of broth, as needed, to adjust the consistency.

6. Taste and season with salt and pepper, then sprinkle with plenty of chopped parsley.

Yield: 4 servings

2 garlic cloves, peeled and minced

Olive oil

1 pound (454 g) chopped (1-inch, or 2.5 cm, pieces) peeled sugar or pie pumpkin or butternut squash, or 1 cup (245 g) pumpkin purée

Vegetable broth for cooking

Juice of 1 lemon

12 ounces (340 g) pancetta or bacon, diced

Salt and fresh-cracked black pepper

1 bunch fresh parsley, chopped

BEST ON:
- Lasagna and cannelloni
- Stuffed pasta (cheese, meat, or vegetables)

GOES WELL ON:
- Al dente penne (or other ridged pasta)
- Cooked meats (hot)
- Crespelle
- Gnocchi
- Rice and risotto

PUMPKIN AND PORCINI SAUCE

Yield: 4 servings

1 shallot, peeled and chopped

1½ tablespoons (21 g) butter

About 10 ounces (280 g) diced peeled sugar or pie pumpkin or butternut squash, or 1 cup (245 g) pumpkin purée

About 10 ounces (280 g) fresh porcini mushrooms, trimmed and diced

¾ cup (180 ml) heavy cream

2 tablespoons (16 g) Soffrito (page 11)

1 bunch fresh parsley, chopped

Salt and fresh-cracked black pepper

1. In a skillet over medium heat, melt the butter. Add the shallot and cook for 2 to 3 minutes until it begins to soften and brown.

2. Add the pumpkin and a splash of water, cover the skillet, and cook for 10 to 15 minutes (if using pumpkin purée, cook just until heated through), stirring occasionally, or until the pumpkin is tender.

3. Add the mushrooms, turn the heat to low, and cook for 10 minutes until the mushrooms are soft.

4. Stir the cream and soffrito into the mushroom mixture, then sprinkle with plenty of chopped parsley.

5. Taste and season with salt and pepper and cook for 3 minutes until the sauce comes together and is heated through.

BEST ON:
- Al dente penne (or other ridged pasta)
- Gnocchi
- Rice and risotto

GOES WELL ON:
- Cooked pasta
- Crespelle
- Lasagna and cannelloni
- Polenta
- Stuffed pasta (cheese, meat, or vegetables)

ZUCCHINI SAUCE

1. Prepare an ice bath.

2. Bring a medium-size saucepan full of salted water to a boil, add the zucchini, and blanch for 1 minute. Drain the zucchini and place it in the ice bath to stop the cooking. Drain again.

3. Return the saucepan to the stovetop over low heat and add the butter to melt.

4. Using a wooden spoon, gradually stir in the cornstarch until coated in the butter.

5. While stirring constantly, slowly trickle in the milk until completely blended.

6. Stir in the zucchini and soffrito. Transfer the sauce to a food processor or blender, or use an immersion blender, and blend until smooth. Return the sauce to the pot and cook over low heat until warm and thickened.

7. Taste and season with salt.

Yield: 4 servings

Salt

1 pound (454 g) zucchini, chopped

7 tablespoons (98 g) butter

½ cup (64 g) cornstarch

2½ cups (600 ml) cold milk

2 tablespoons (16 g) Soffrito (page 11)

BEST ON:
- Lasagna and cannelloni

GOES WELL ON:
- Cooked meats and fish (hot or cold)
- Cooked pasta (all types)
- Crespelle
- Eggs
- Gnocchi
- Polenta
- Raw meats and fish: tartare and carpaccio
- Rice and risotto
- Stuffed pasta (cheese, meat, seafood, or vegetables)

ZUCCHINI, BRIE, AND PINE NUT SAUCE

Yield: 4 servings

¾ cup (105 g) pine nuts

2 salt-packed anchovies

2 shallots, peeled and chopped

About 10 ounces (280 g) zucchini, chopped

1½ tablespoons (21 g) butter

¾ cup (180 ml) heavy cream

1 cup (150 g) Brie or Camembert cheese

Salt and fresh-cracked black pepper

BEST ON:
- Cooked pasta (all types)
- Gnocchi

GOES WELL ON:
- Boiled potatoes
- Lasagna and cannelloni
- Polenta risotto

1. In a small nonstick skillet over medium-high heat, toast the pine nuts for 2 to 3 minutes until lightly browned and fragrant. Set aside.

2. Remove any bones, heads, and tails from the anchovies and rinse them under running water.

3. In a skillet over medium heat, melt the butter. Add the shallots and anchovies and cook for 2 to 3 minutes, or until the shallots begin to brown and the anchovies melt.

4. Add the zucchini, turn the heat to low, and cook for 5 minutes, stirring occasionally.

5. Stir in the cream, the Brie in pieces, and toasted pine nuts. Cook, stirring, until the cheese melts and the sauce is heated through.

6. Taste and season with salt and pepper.

2
EVERYBODY LOVES PESTO

CLASSIC PESTO

Yield: 6 to 8 servings

1 handful pine nuts

1 garlic clove, peeled, or
    more as needed

4 ounces (112 g) grated grana
    (such as Asiago or
    Grana Padano)

2 ounces (55 g) grated
    Parmigiano-Reggiano or
    Pecorino Romano cheese

3 cups packed (120 g)
    Ligurian or sweet Italian
    basil leaves, cleaned with
    dampened cloth

3 tablespoons (45 ml) olive oil

1½ tablespoons (21 g) butter,
    at room temperature

1. Place a blender container or the bowl of a food processor and blade in the freezer for a couple of hours—the cold of the freezer plus the ice added in step 5 will reduce oxidation of the basil.

2. In a small nonstick skillet over medium-high heat, toast the pine nuts for 2 to 3 minutes until lightly browned and fragrant. Set aside.

3. In the chilled blender, combine the pine nuts, garlic clove, or more cloves to taste, cheeses, and basil leaves. Add the oil and 1 ice cube and pulse until you have a finely chopped sauce. Transfer the pesto to a bowl and stir in the butter until emulsified.

4. Taste and season with salt.

BEST ON:
- Al dente pasta
- Bruschetta and crostini
- Gnocchi

GOES WELL ON:
- Boiled potatoes
- Cooked meats and fish
  (hot or cold)
- Cooked vegetables
- Eggs
- Pasta salad
- Pizza, focaccia, piadina
- Raw meats and fish:
  tartare and carpaccio
- Rice and risotto
- Rice salad
- Veloutés and cream soups

CREAM PESTO

1. In a food processor or blender, or a medium-size bowl and using an immersion blender, combine the basil, grana, Pecorino Romano, pine nuts, walnuts, and cream.

2. Blend quickly, drizzling in the oil until you have a pesto consistency.

3. Taste and season with salt.

Yield: 4 to 6 servings

1 pound (454 g) fresh basil leaves

1 cup (100 g) grated grana (such as Asiago, Grana Padano, or Parmigiano-Reggiano)

1 cup (100 g) grated Pecorino Romano cheese

¾ cup (105 g) pine nuts

¾ cup (75 g) walnuts

3 tablespoons (45 ml) heavy cream

Olive oil

Salt

BEST ON:
- Cooked pasta (all types)
- Cooked meats and fish (hot or cold)

GOES WELL ON:
- Bruschetta and crostini
- Crustaceans
- Gnocchi
- Pasta salad
- Pizza, focaccia, piadina
- Raw meats and fish: tartare and carpaccio
- Rice salad
- Stewed legumes
- Veloutés and cream soups

ASPARAGUS PESTO

Yield: 4 servings

Olive oil

1 garlic clove, peeled

About 10 ounces (280 g) asparagus, cut into small pieces

¾ cup (105 g) pine nuts

½ cup (50 g) grated grana (such as Asiago, Parmigiano-Reggiano, or Pecorino Romano)

1 bunch fresh basil

Salt

BEST ON:
- Al dente pasta
- Rice and risotto
- Stuffed pasta (cheese or vegetables)

GOES WELL ON:
- Boiled potatoes
- Cooked meats and fish (cold)
- Eggs
- Gnocchi
- Lasagna and cannelloni
- Pasta salad
- Raw meats and fish: tartare and carpaccio
- Rice salad

1. Pour a few swirls of oil into a skillet and add the garlic clove and asparagus stalk pieces. Add enough water to just cover and cook over medium-high heat for 2 to 3 minutes until the asparagus is crisp-tender and most of the water has evaporated. Transfer to a food processor or blender, or use an immersion blender, and add the pine nuts, grana, and basil.

2. Blend quickly, trickling in more oil until you have a pesto consistency.

3. Taste and season with salt.

ARTICHOKE PESTO

Yield: 4 servings

1. Cook the artichoke hearts according to the package directions until tender. Drain and transfer to a food processor or blender, or use an immersion blender, add a swirl or two of oil, and blend until smooth, adding more oil as needed.

2. Add the pine nuts, grana, and basil.

3. Blend quickly, trickling in a bit more oil until you have a pesto consistency.

4. Taste and season with salt.

1 pound (454 g) frozen artichoke hearts

Olive oil

¾ cup (105 g) pine nuts

½ cup (50 g) grated grana (such as Asiago, Parmigiano-Reggiano, or Pecorino Romano)

1 bunch fresh basil

Salt

BEST ON:
- Al dente pasta
- Pasta salad

GOES WELL ON:
- Bruschetta and crostini
- Cooked meats and fish (cold)
- Cooked vegetables (served room temperature)
- Gnocchi
- Pizza, focaccia, piadina
- Raw meats and fish: tartare and carpaccio
- Rice and risotto
- Veloutés and cream soups

BROAD BEAN, ALMOND, AND PINE NUT PESTO

Yield: 4 to 6 servings

8 ounces (225 g) shelled fresh broad (fava) beans

¾ cup (105 g) pine nuts

1 cup (150 g) grated ricotta salata or feta cheese

⅓ cup (48 g) peeled almonds

1 bunch fresh basil

Olive oil

Salt

BEST ON:
- Pasta salad
- Stuffed pasta (cheese, meat, seafood, or vegetables, served room temperature)

GOES WELL ON:
- Bruschetta and crostini
- Cooked meats and fish (cold)
- Cooked vegetables (served room temperature)
- Gnocchi
- Lasagna and cannelloni
- Raw meats and fish: tartare and carpaccio
- Rice salad

1. Prepare an ice bath.

2. Bring a saucepan full of water to a boil. Add the broad beans and blanch for 2 minutes. Drain and transfer to the ice bath to stop the cooking. Drain again and remove the outer skins.

3. In a small nonstick skillet over medium-high heat, toast the pine nuts for 2 to 3 minutes until lightly browned and fragrant. Let cool slightly, then transfer the pine nuts to a food processor or blender, or to a medium-size bowl and use an immersion blender.

4. Add the broad beans, ricotta salata, almonds, and basil.

5. Blend quickly, trickling in the oil until you have a pesto consistency.

6. Taste and season with salt.

BROCCOLI PESTO

Yield: 4 servings

½ cup (70 g) pine nuts

Salt

12 ounces (340 g) broccoli
florets, cut into small chunks

½ cup (50 g) walnuts

1 bunch fresh basil, leaves only

½ cup (50 g) grated
Parmigiano-Reggiano
cheese

Olive oil

BEST ON:
- Bruschetta and crostini
- Cooked meats and fish
  (hot or cold)
- Cooked vegetables
- Pasta salad

GOES WELL ON:
- Eggs
- Gnocchi
- Rice salad
- Stewed legumes
- Veloutés and cream soups

1. In a small nonstick skillet over medium-high heat, toast the pine nuts for 2 to 3 minutes until lightly browned and fragrant. Set aside.

2. Prepare an ice bath.

3. Bring a large saucepan full of salted water to a boil, add the broccoli, and blanch for 2 to 3 minutes until crisp-tender. Drain the broccoli and place it in the ice bath to stop the cooking. Drain the broccoli again and transfer it to a food processor or blender, or return it to the bowl and use an immersion blender.

4. While blending, add the following ingredients, in this order, blending after each addition: toasted pine nuts, walnuts, basil leaves, cheese, and olive oil. Blend until the pesto is smooth, adding more oil as needed.

5. Taste and season with salt.

SICILIAN PESTO

Yield: 4 to 6 servings

4 ounces (115 g)
   cherry tomatoes

8 ounces (225 g) ricotta
   (preferably sheep's milk)

¾ cup (105 g) pine nuts

1 cup (145 g) almonds

1 bunch fresh basil

½ cup (50 g) grated grana
   (such as Grana Padano
   or Parmigiano-Reggiano)

½ cup (50 g) grated Pecorino
   Romano cheese

Olive oil

Salt and fresh-cracked
   black pepper

1. Prepare an ice bath. If the tomatoes are large enough, score them with an X on the bottom to make them easier to peel. Bring a large pot of water to a boil, add the tomatoes, and cook for about 1 minute, or until the skins start to peel back in the place where you scored them. Using a slotted spoon, transfer the tomatoes to the ice bath. When cool enough to handle, peel the tomatoes.

2. In a food processor or blender, or in a medium-size bowl using an immersion blender, combine the tomatoes, ricotta, pine nuts, almonds, basil, grana, and Pecorino Romano.

3. Blend quickly, trickling in the oil until you have a pesto consistency.

4. Taste and season with salt and pepper.

BEST ON:
- Cooked pasta
  (all types)
- Pasta salad

GOES WELL ON:
- Bruschetta and crostini
- Cooked meats and fish
  (served cold)
- Eggs
- Lasagna and cannelloni
- Raw meats and fish:
  tartare and carpaccio
- Rice salad
- Stuffed pasta
  (meat, seafood, or vegetables)

BROAD BEAN PESTO

Yield: 4 servings

1. In a food processor or blender, or in a medium-size bowl and using an immersion blender, combine the beans, cheese, mint, and garlic.

2. Blend quickly, trickling in the oil until you have a thick, smooth consistency, being careful not to heat the pesto while blending. Transfer the sauce to a bowl.

3. Taste and season with salt and pepper.

1 cup (170 g) shelled fresh
    baby broad (fava) beans

⅓ cup (33 g) grated semi-aged
    Pecorino Romano cheese

2 fresh mint leaves

1 garlic clove, peeled

Olive oil

Salt and fresh-cracked
    black pepper

BEST ON:
- Bruschetta and crostini
- Pasta salad

GOES WELL ON:
- Cooked meats and fish
  (hot or cold)
- Crustaceans
- Pizza, focaccia, piadina
- Raw meats and fish:
  tartare and carpaccio
- Rice salad
- Veloutés and cream soups

3

A TREASURY OF ToMATO SAUCES

CLASSIC TOMATO SAUCE

Yield: 4 servings

Olive oil

3 large garlic cloves, unpeeled

1 pound (454 g) not-too-ripe
    mixed fresh tomatoes
    (such as beefsteak, cherry,
    Roma), roughly chopped

Fresh oregano leaves
    for seasoning

Salt and fresh-cracked
    black pepper

BEST ON:
- Cooked pasta (all types)
- Lasagna and cannelloni
- Stuffed pasta (cheese, meat,
  seafood, or vegetables)

GOES WELL ON:
- Bruschetta and crostini
- Cooked meats and
  fish (hot)
- Crespelle
- Crustaceans
- Gnocchi
- Pizza, focaccia, piadina
- Polenta
- Stewed legumes

1. Pour a few swirls of oil into a skillet and add the unpeeled garlic cloves. Sauté over medium heat for 2 to 3 minutes until they soften and begin to brown. Crush the garlic with a wooden spoon, stir it into the oil to flavor it, then remove and discard the garlic.

2. Add the tomatoes to the skillet and sauté for 5 minutes, stirring to help break up the tomatoes.

3. Sprinkle with oregano to taste and stir to combine.

4. Taste and season with salt and pepper.

SUPER RED
ToMATO SAUCE

1. If using fresh tomatoes, prepare an ice bath. Score the tomatoes with an X on the bottom to make them easier to peel. Bring a large pot of water to a boil, add the tomatoes, and cook for about 1 minute, or until the skins start to peel back in the place where you scored them. Using a slotted spoon, transfer the tomatoes to the ice bath. When cool enough to handle, peel the tomatoes, halve them, remove the seeds, and cut them into strips.

2. Pour a few generous swirls of oil into a saucepan and add the unpeeled garlic cloves. Sauté over medium heat for 2 to 3 minutes until softened and beginning to brown. Crush the garlic with a wooden spoon, stir it into the oil to flavor it, then remove and discard the garlic.

3. In a small bowl, stir together the tomato paste and ½ cup (120 ml) of water until the tomato paste dissolves. Add it to the saucepan, along with the tomatoes and tomato purée.

4. Stir the basil into the sauce with the remaining ½ cup (120 ml) of water. Cover the pan loosely and simmer for 1 hour, adding more water if the sauce become dry.

5. Taste and season with salt and pepper.

Yield: 4 servings

1 pound (454 g) fresh San Marzano or Roma tomatoes, or 1 (14.5-ounce, or 410 g) can whole peeled San Marzano tomatoes

Olive oil

2 large garlic cloves, unpeeled

½ cup (130 g) tomato paste

1 cup (240 ml) water, divided, plus more as needed

1 cup (250 g) tomato purée

1 bunch fresh basil, chopped

Salt and fresh-cracked black pepper

BEST ON:
• Everything

GOES WELL ON:
• Everything

TUSCAN-STYLE RED TOMATO SAUCE

Yield: 4 servings

1 pound (454 g) fresh San Marzano or Roma tomatoes, or 1 (14.5-ounce, or 410 g) can whole peeled San Marzano tomatoes

2 large red onions, thinly sliced

Olive oil

2 fresh bay leaves

Salt and fresh-cracked black pepper

BEST ON:

- Cooked pasta (all types)
- Cooked meats and fish (hot)
- Stuffed pasta (cheese, meat, seafood, or vegetables)

GOES WELL ON:

- Bruschetta and crostini
- Crustaceans
- Eggs
- Gnocchi
- Lasagna and cannelloni
- Polenta
- Raw meats and fish: tartare and carpaccio
- Stewed legumes

1. If using fresh tomatoes, prepare an ice bath. Score the tomatoes with an X on the bottom to make them easier to peel. Bring a large pot of water to a boil, add the tomatoes, and cook for about 1 minute, or until the skins start to peel back in the place where you scored them. Using a slotted spoon, transfer the tomatoes to the ice bath. When cool enough to handle, peel the tomatoes, halve them, remove the seeds, and cut them into strips.

2. Add the onions to a large skillet. Pour in a few swirls of oil and add the bay leaves. Sauté over medium heat for about 5 minutes until the onions begin to soften.

3. Stir in the tomatoes, turn the heat to low, and simmer the sauce for about 20 minutes until thickened, stirring occasionally to help break up the tomatoes. Remove and discard the bay leaves.

4. Taste and season with salt and pepper and finish with a drizzle of oil.

ToMATO SAUCE WITH OLIVES, CAPERS, AND PINE NUTS

Yield: 4 to 6 servings

¾ cup (105 g) pine nuts

1 pound (454 g) fresh San Marzano or Roma tomatoes, or 1 (14.5-ounce, or 410 g) can whole peeled San Marzano tomatoes

Olive oil

1 red onion, thinly sliced

1 bunch fresh basil, coarsely chopped

2 tablespoons (18 g) salt-packed capers, rinsed and coarsely chopped

1 cup pitted green olives, coarsely chopped

¼ cup (33 g) Soffrito (page 11)

Salt and fresh-cracked black pepper

1. In a small nonstick skillet over medium-high heat, toast the pine nuts for 2 to 3 minutes until lightly browned and fragrant. Set aside.

2. If using fresh tomatoes, prepare an ice bath. Score the tomatoes with an X on the bottom to make them easier to peel. Bring a large pot of water to a boil, add the tomatoes, and cook for about 1 minute, or until the skins start to peel back in the place where you scored them. Using a slotted spoon, transfer the tomatoes to the ice bath. When cool enough to handle, peel the tomatoes, halve them, remove the seeds, and cut them into strips.

3. Pour a few swirls of oil into a saucepan and add the onion. Sauté over medium heat for about 5 minutes until the onion softens and begins to brown.

4. Add the tomatoes and simmer for 15 minutes, stirring occasionally. Transfer to a food processor or blender, or use an immersion blender, and blend until smooth. Return the sauce to the pan.

5. Add the basil, capers, and olives to the sauce. Stir in the soffrito. Cook for 5 minutes to warm through and thicken slightly. Stir in the pine nuts. Taste and season with salt and pepper.

BEST ON:
- Cooked pasta (all types)
- Stuffed pasta (cheese, meat, seafood, or vegetables)

GOES WELL ON:
- Boiled potatoes
- Bruschetta and crostini
- Cooked vegetables
- Gnocchi
- Pizza, focaccia, piadina
- Polenta
- Stewed legumes

PUTTANESCA SAUCE

1. Pour a few swirls of oil into a skillet and add the garlic cloves. Sauté over medium heat for 2 to 3 minutes until softened and browned.

2. Add the anchovies to the skillet. Cook, stirring with a wooden spoon until they have melted.

3. Add the olives to the skillet, along with the soffrito and capers. Stir to combine.

4. Add the tomatoes. Turn the heat to low and gently simmer for 20 minutes, stirring occasionally to break up the tomatoes, until the sauce is slightly thickened. Stir in the parsley.

5. Taste and season with salt and pepper.

Yield: 2 to 4 servings

Olive oil

4 garlic cloves, peeled

4 oil-packed anchovy fillets, chopped, or 2 teaspoons anchovy paste

¾ cup (75 g) pitted Gaeta olives or other black olives, chopped

¼ cup (33 g) Soffrito (page 11)

1 tablespoon (9 g) salt-packed capers, rinsed

8 ounces (225 g) peeled whole tomatoes, fresh or canned

1 tablespoon (4 g) fresh parsley, chopped

Salt and fresh-cracked black pepper

BEST ON:
- Cooked pasta (all types)

GOES WELL ON:
- Boiled potatoes
- Bruschetta and crostini
- Eggs
- Gnocchi
- Lasagna and cannelloni

SPICY ToMATO SAUCE WITH RED ONIONS

Yield: 6 servings

1⅓ pounds (605 g) fresh San Marzano or Roma tomatoes, or about 8 whole peeled San Marzano tomatoes from a 28-ounce (794 g) can (saving the remaining canned tomatoes for another use)

Olive oil

1⅓ pounds (605 g) red onions, thinly sliced

1 bunch fresh thyme, stems removed

¼ cup (33 g) Soffrito (page 11)

1 teaspoon red pepper flakes, plus more as needed

Salt

1. If using fresh tomatoes, prepare an ice bath. Score the tomatoes with an X on the bottom to make them easier to peel. Bring a large pot of water to a boil, add the tomatoes, and cook for about 1 minute, or until the skins start to peel back in the place where you scored them. Using a slotted spoon, transfer the tomatoes to the ice bath. When cool enough to handle, peel the tomatoes, halve them, remove the seeds, and cut them into strips.

2. Pour a few swirls of oil into a saucepan and add the onions and thyme. Sauté over medium heat for 10 minutes until softened and translucent.

3. Stir in the tomatoes, soffrito, and red pepper flakes. Simmer for 30 minutes, stirring occasionally to help break up the tomatoes, adding a little water if the sauce becomes dry.

4. Taste and season with salt and add more red pepper flakes to taste.

BEST ON:
- Cooked pasta (all types)
- Stuffed pasta (cheese, meat, seafood, or vegetables)

GOES WELL ON:
- Boiled potatoes
- Bruschetta and crostini
- Cooked meats and fish (hot or cold)
- Cooked vegetables
- Crespelle
- Gnocchi
- Lasagna and cannelloni
- Pizza, focaccia, piadina
- Polenta
- Raw meats and fish: tartare and carpaccio
- Stewed legumes

ARRABBIATA SAUCE

Yield: 4 servings

1 pound (454 g) fresh tomatoes, or 1 (14.5-ounce, or 410 g) can whole peeled tomatoes

Olive oil

2 large garlic cloves, crushed

1 to 2 teaspoons red pepper flakes, plus more as needed

¾ cup (75 g) grated grana (such as Asiago, Parmigiano-Reggiano, or Pecorino Romano)

Salt and black pepper

BEST ON:
- Al dente penne pasta (or other ridged pasta)
- Lasagna and cannelloni

GOES WELL ON:
- Cooked meats (hot; such as beef, chicken, or pork)
- Crespelle
- Eggs
- Gnocchi
- Pizza, focaccia, piadina
- Polenta
- Stewed legumes
- Stuffed pasta (cheese, meat, or vegetables)
- Veloutés and cream soups

1. If using fresh tomatoes, prepare an ice bath. Score the tomatoes with an X on the bottom to make them easier to peel. Bring a large pot of water to a boil, add the tomatoes, and cook for about 1 minute, or until the skins start to peel back in the place where you scored them. Using a slotted spoon, transfer the tomatoes to the ice bath. When cool enough to handle, peel the tomatoes, halve them, remove the seeds, and dice them.

2. Pour a few swirls of oil into a nonstick skillet. Add the garlic cloves and red pepper flakes to taste and sauté over medium heat for 1 to 2 minutes until softened and fragrant, being careful not to burn the garlic.

3. Add the tomatoes and cook for 1 minute.

4. Stir in the cheese. If the sauce is for a pasta, add the cheese after dressing the pasta.

5. Taste and season with salt and pepper, adding more red pepper flakes for a spicier sauce. Remove and discard the garlic, then serve.

BYZANTIUM SAUCE

Yield: 4 to 6 servings

1⅓ pounds (605 g) cherry
  tomatoes, roughly chopped

2 cups (490 g) Tomato Sauce
  (page 98), or store-bought

¼ cup (60 ml) olive oil, plus
  more as needed

2 bunches fresh basil, finely
  chopped with stems
  removed

4 garlic cloves, peeled
  and minced

Salt

Red pepper flakes
  for seasoning

BEST ON:
- Al dente pasta
- Bruschetta and crostini
- Cooked meats (cold)
- Pasta salad
- Pizza, focaccia, piadina

GOES WELL ON:
- Cooked fish (cold)
- Eggs
- Gnocchi
- Polenta
- Raw meats and fish:
  tartare and carpaccio
- Veloutés and cream soups

1. In a large bowl, stir together the chopped tomatoes and
   tomato sauce.

2. Slowly pour in the oil in a steady stream, stirring to blend,
   until the mixture is emulsified.

3. Stir in the basil and garlic.

4. Taste and season with salt and red pepper flakes and
   drizzle with more oil, if desired.

CAPRESE SAUCE

Yield: 4 to 6 servings

1 pound (454 g) cherry tomatoes, diced

About 10 ounces (280 g) fresh mozzarella cheese, diced

Olive oil

Salt and fresh-cracked black pepper

1 bunch fresh basil

BEST ON:
- Al dente pasta
- Bruschetta and crostini
- Gnocchi

GOES WELL ON:
- Cooked meats and fish (cold)
- Eggs
- Pasta salad
- Pizza, focaccia, piadina
- Raw meats and fish: tartare and carpaccio
- Rice and risotto
- Rice salad

1. Place the tomatoes in a colander set over a bowl and let drain for 20 minutes.

2. Place the mozzarella in another colander set over a bowl and let drain for 20 minutes.

3. In a medium-size bowl, gently stir together the drained cherry tomatoes and mozzarella.

4. Season with a generous drizzle or two of oil and salt and pepper to taste.

5. Tear the basil leaves into pieces and stir them into the sauce.

SPICY TOMATO SAUCE

Yield: 4 servings

1. If using fresh tomatoes, prepare an ice bath. Score the tomatoes with an X on the bottom to make them easier to peel. Bring a large pot of water to a boil, add the tomatoes, and cook for about 1 minute, or until the skins start to peel back in the place where you scored them. Using a slotted spoon, transfer the tomatoes to the ice bath. When cool enough to handle, peel the tomatoes.

2. Pour a few swirls of oil into a saucepan and add the tomatoes, chile to taste, onion, and garlic. Cook over low heat for 15 minutes until the vegetables are soft and the sauce is thickened, stirring occasionally to break up the tomatoes.

3. Stir in the parsley.

4. Taste and season with salt and pepper.

1 pound (454 g) fresh tomatoes, or 1 (14.5-ounce, or 410 g) can whole peeled tomatoes

Olive oil

1 fresh hot chile pepper (such as habanero or Scotch bonnet), seed and diced

1 large white onion, minced

3 garlic cloves, peeled and minced

1 bunch fresh parsley, chopped

Salt and fresh-cracked black pepper

BEST ON:
- Bruschetta and crostini
- Cooked pasta (all types)
- Pizza, focaccia, piadina
- Stuffed pasta (cheese, meat, seafood, or vegetables)

GOES WELL ON:
- Boiled potatoes
- Cooked meats and fish (hot or cold)

- Cooked vegetables
- Crustaceans
- Eggs
- Gnocchi
- Lasagna and cannelloni
- Pasta salad
- Polenta
- Raw meats and fish: tartare and carpaccio
- Rice and risotto
- Rice salad

NEAPOLITAN ToMATO-BASIL SAUCE

Yield: 4 servings

1 pound (454 g) fresh San
  Marzano or Roma tomatoes,
  or 1 (14.5-ounce, or 410 g)
  can whole peeled San
  Marzano tomatoes

Olive oil

2 large garlic cloves, unpeeled

Salt and fresh-cracked
  black pepper

1 bunch fresh basil

BEST ON:
- Cooked pasta (all types)

GOES WELL ON:
- Bruschetta and crostini
- Cooked meats and fish
  (hot or cold)
- Crespelle
- Crustaceans
- Egg pasta dressed
- Gnocchi
- Lasagna and cannelloni
- Pasta salad
- Pizza, focaccia, piadina
- Polenta
- Raw meats and fish:
  tartare and carpaccio
- Stuffed pasta (cheese, meat,
  seafood, or vegetables)

1. If using fresh tomatoes, prepare an ice bath. Score the tomatoes with an X on the bottom to make them easier to peel. Bring a large pot of water to a boil, add the tomatoes, and cook for about 1 minute, or until the skins start to peel back in the place where you scored them. Using a slotted spoon, transfer the tomatoes to the ice bath. When cool enough to handle, peel the tomatoes, halve them, remove the seeds, and cut them into strips.

2. Pour a few swirls of oil into a saucepan and add the unpeeled garlic cloves. Sauté over medium heat for 2 to 3 minutes until softened and browned, being careful not to burn the garlic. Crush the garlic with a wooden spoon, stir it into the oil to flavor it, then remove and discard the garlic.

3. Add the tomatoes, turn the heat to low, and simmer for 25 minutes, stirring occasionally to help break up the tomatoes.

4. Taste and season with salt and pepper.

5. Chop the basil and stir it into the sauce. Finish with a drizzle of oil.

4

CHEESE
SAUCES AND
EGG SAUCES

CHECCA MOZZARELLA SAUCE

Yield: 6 servings

8 ounces (225 g) mozzarella cheese, cubed

5⅓ ounces (151 g) caciotta or Pecorino Romano cheese, cubed

Olive oil

Salt and fresh-cracked black pepper

5 fresh red oxheart or beefsteak tomatoes, cubed

1 bunch fresh basil, chopped

BEST ON:
- Al dente pasta
- Stuffed pasta (cheese, meat, or vegetables)

GOES WELL ON:
- Bruschetta and crostini
- Cooked vegetables
- Gnocchi
- Pizza, focaccia, piadina

1. Place the mozzarella and caciotta in a large bowl.

2. Season with a few swirls of oil and salt and pepper to taste.

3. Add the tomatoes to the mozzarella and caciotta.

4. Add the basil to the sauce. Gently stir to combine.

5. Taste and season with more oil, salt, and pepper, as needed.

BRIE, ZUCCHINI BLOSSOM, AND ANCHOVY SAUCE

Yield: 4 to 6 servings

3 salt-packed anchovies, or
    1½ teaspoons anchovy paste

1½ tablespoons (21 g) butter

2 shallots, peeled and chopped

About 10 ounces (280 g)
    zucchini blossoms, coarsely
    chopped

¾ cup (180 ml) heavy cream

8 ounces (225 g) Brie cheese

Salt and fresh-cracked
    black pepper

BEST ON:
- Al dente penne
  (or other ridged pasta)
- Pizza, focaccia, piadina

GOES WELL ON:
- Bruschetta and crostini
- Cooked meat and fish
  (hot or cold)
- Cooked pasta (any type)
- Cooked vegetables
- Gnocchi
- Lasagna and cannelloni
- Stuffed pasta (cheese, meat,
  seafood, or vegetables)

1. Remove any bones, heads, and tails from the anchovies and rinse them under running water.

2. In a skillet, melt the butter over medium heat. Add the shallots and anchovies and cook for 3 to 4 minutes, stirring occasionally, until the shallots begin to brown.

3. Add the zucchini blossoms, turn the heat to low, and cook for 2 minutes. Transfer the mixture to a food processor or blender, or use an immersion blender, and blend until smooth.

4. Pour in the cream, add the Brie in pieces, and blend again until mostly smooth.

5. Return the sauce to the pan over low heat and let the cheese melt and the sauce thicken for about 5 minutes.

6. Taste and season with salt and pepper.

SPICY SIX-CHEESE SAUCE

1. Transfer the cheeses to a saucepan.

2. Add the butter and pour in the milk and Cognac. Cook over low heat until the cheeses melt and the sauce comes together, stirring occasionally.

3. Taste and season with cinnamon, crushed garlic cloves, grated nutmeg, and salt.

Yield: 4 to 6 servings

3½ ounces (100 g) Gruyère cheese, grated

3 ounces (85 g) smoked provola or provolone cheese, grated

3 ounces (85 g) Pecorino Romano cheese, grated

3 ounces (85 g) mozzarella cheese, grated

1¾ ounces (49 g) fontina cheese, grated

1½ ounces (43 g) grana (such as Asiago or Parmigiano-Reggiano), grated

3 tablespoons (42 g) butter

1⅔ cups (400 ml) milk

1 tablespoon (15 ml) Cognac

Ground cinnamon for seasoning

Garlic cloves, crushed, for seasoning

Freshly grated nutmeg for seasoning

Salt

BEST ON:
- Cooked pasta (all types)
- Gnocchi
- Rice and risotto

GOES WELL ON:
- Boiled potatoes
- Bruschetta and crostini
- Cooked meats (hot)
- Cooked vegetables
- Crespelle
- Lasagna and cannelloni
- Polenta

FOUR-CHEESE SAUCE

Yield: 4 to 6 servings

3½ ounces (100 g) Gruyère
cheese, grated

3½ ounces (100 g) fontina
cheese, grated

3½ ounces (100 g) grana
(such as Asiago,
Parmigiano-Reggiano, or
Pecorino Romano), grated

3 ounces (85 g) sharp
provolone cheese, grated

3½ tablespoons (49 g) butter

1⅔ cups (400 ml) milk

BEST ON:
- Cooked pasta (all types)
- Gnocchi
- Rice and risotto

GOES WELL ON:
- Boiled potatoes
- Bruschetta and crostini
- Cooked meats (hot)
- Cooked vegetables
- Crespelle
- Lasagna and cannelloni
- Polenta

1. Transfer the cheeses to a small saucepan.

2. Add the butter and pour in the milk. Cook over low heat until the cheeses melt and the sauce comes together, stirring occasionally.

3. If desired, this sauce can be enriched, off the heat, with fresh-cracked black pepper, crushed Sichuan peppercorns, grated walnuts, ground cinnamon, ground cloves, and other spices you prefer.

BRIE AND PEPPER SAUCE

1. Transfer the brie to a saucepan.

2. Pour in the cream and milk and add the butter. Cook over low heat for about 5 minutes until the cheese melts and the sauce thickens.

3. Taste and season generously with white pepper.

Yield: 4 to 6 servings

12 ounces (340 g) Brie cheese, finely chopped

1½ cups (360 ml) heavy cream

½ cup (120 ml) milk

3 tablespoons (42 g) butter

Ground white pepper

BEST ON:
- Al dente penne (or other ridged pasta)
- Gnocchi
- Rice and risotto

GOES WELL ON:
- Boiled potatoes
- Bruschetta and crostini
- Cooked vegetables
- Crespelle
- Eggs
- Lasagna and cannelloni
- Pizza, focaccia, piadina
- Stuffed pasta (cheese or vegetables)

GRANA AND SPECK SAUCE

Yield: 4 to 6 servings

12 ounces (340 g) grated grana (such as Asiago, Parmigiano-Reggiano, or Pecorino Romano)

3 tablespoons (42 g) butter

1½ cups (360 ml) heavy cream

½ cup (120 ml) milk

1 (8-ounce, or 225 g) piece speck, prosciutto, or bacon, finely chopped

Fresh-cracked pepper

BEST ON:
- Al dente penne (or other ridged pasta)
- Gnocchi

GOES WELL ON:
- Boiled potatoes
- Cooked pasta (all types)
- Cooked vegetables
- Crespelle
- Lasagna and cannelloni
- Polenta
- Rice and risotto

I. In a small saucepan, stir together the grana, butter, cream, and milk. Cook over low heat for about 10 minutes, stirring occasionally, until the sauce is heated and smooth.

2. Stir in the speck and cook for 1 to 2 minutes more to warm it.

3. Taste and season generously with pepper.

GORGONZOLA AND WALNUT SAUCE

1. Add the gorgonzola and walnuts to a small saucepan and pour in the cream and milk. Cook over low heat until the cheese melts, then simmer for about 5 minutes to thicken the sauce.

2. Taste and season with salt and generously with pepper.

Yield: 4 to 6 servings

12 ounces (340 g) Gorgonzola cheese, finely chopped

1 cup (100 g) shelled walnuts, coarsely chopped

¾ cup (180 ml) heavy cream

½ cup (120 ml) milk

Salt and fresh-cracked black pepper

BEST ON:
- Al dente pasta
- Cooked beef (hot)

GOES WELL ON:
- Bruschetta and crostini
- Cooked vegetables
- Gnocchi
- Lasagna and cannelloni
- Polenta
- Rice and risotto
- Stuffed pasta (cheese or vegetables)

GORGONZOLA AND PEAR SAUCE

Yield: 4 to 6 servings

12 ounces (340 g)
   Gorgonzola cheese,
   finely chopped

¾ cup (94 g) coarsely
   chopped peeled pear

¾ cup (180 ml) heavy cream

½ cup (120 ml) milk

Salt and fresh-cracked
   black pepper

BEST ON:
- Al dente pasta
- Cooked beef (hot)

GOES WELL ON:
- Bruschetta and crostini
- Cooked vegetables
- Gnocchi
- Lasagna and cannelloni
- Polenta
- Rice and risotto
- Stuffed pasta
  (cheese or vegetables)

1. Add the Gorgonzola to a small saucepan.

2. Add the chopped pears and pour in the cream and milk.
Cook over low heat until the cheese melts, then simmer for
about 5 minutes to thicken the sauce.

3. Taste and season with salt and generously with pepper.

RICOTTA SAUCE

Yield: 6 to 8 servings

1. Place the walnuts in a medium-size bowl.

2. Add the ricotta. Season with salt and pepper to taste and a generous drizzle of oil.

3. Whisk vigorously until blended.

1½ cups (150 g) walnuts or hazelnuts, finely chopped

1 pound (454 g) ricotta cheese (preferably sheep's milk)

Salt and fresh-cracked black pepper

Olive oil

BEST ON:
- Bruschetta and crostini
- Veloutés and cream soups

GOES WELL ON:
- Gnocchi
- Lasagna and cannelloni
- Pasta salad
- Pizza, focaccia, piadina

RICOTTA AND SALAMI SAUCE

Yield: 4 to 6 servings

1 pound (454 g) ricotta
(preferably sheep's milk)

1 bunch fresh parsley, finely
chopped

⅔ cup (100 g) salami

Fresh-cracked black pepper

BEST ON:
- Lasagna and cannelloni

GOES WELL ON:
- Al dente pasta
- Bruschetta and crostini
- Eggs
- Gnocchi
- Pizza, focaccia, piadina
- Veloutés and cream soups

1. Place the salami in a food processor and pulse until finely chopped.

2. In a large bowl, combine the ricotta, parsley, and salami. Season with pepper.

3. Whisk vigorously until combined and creamy.

SIMPLE CHEESE AND EGGS

Yield: 4 servings

2 tablespoons (30 ml)
    olive oil

2 garlic cloves, unpeeled

¾ cup (75 g) grated Pecorino
    Romano cheese

4 large eggs

Salt and fresh-cracked
    black pepper

BEST ON:
• Cooked pasta (all types)

GOES WELL ON:
• Gnocchi
• Rice

1. In a skillet over medium heat, combine the oil and unpeeled garlic cloves. Cook for 2 to 3 minutes, stirring occasionally, until softened and golden brown. Smash the garlic cloves, then remove and discard them.

2. In a large bowl, beat the eggs and season with salt and pepper to taste.

3. Whisk in the cheese and garlic oil until blended.

4. When dressing the hot pasta with the sauce, which will cook the eggs gently from its residual heat, add about ½ cup (120 ml) of the pasta cooking water, as needed, for a creamier texture. If you're concerned about uncooked egg, combine everything in the skillet and cook gently over low heat for about 1 minute, stirring constantly, to cook the egg.

ToMATO OMELET SAUCE

Yield: 4 to 6 servings

1. In a large bowl, whisk the eggs until blended. Add the chives, cherry tomatoes, string cheese, and grana. Season with a pinch of nutmeg and salt and pepper to taste and whisk to combine.

2. Pour a few swirls of oil into a skillet, tilting the pan to coat the bottom. Pour in the beaten egg mixture and cook over medium heat until the eggs are set. Gently flip the omelet and cook until the other side is set. Remove from the pan, let cool, and cut the omelet into strips.

3. Place the soffrito in a saucepan and pour the tomato purée over it. Add the omelet strips. Cook over high heat for 10 minutes, stirring frequently, to reduce and thicken the sauce.

4. Taste and season with salt and pepper.

6 eggs

1 bunch fresh chives, finely chopped

4 ounces (115 g) cherry tomatoes, finely chopping

8 ounces (225 g) string cheese, cubed

4 ounces (115 g) grated grana (such as Asiago, Parmigiano-Reggiano, or Pecorino Romano)

Freshly grated nutmeg for seasoning

Olive oil

2 tablespoons (16 g) Soffrito (page 11)

2¼ cups (563 g) tomato purée

Salt and fresh-cracked black pepper

BEST ON:
- Cooked pasta (all types)
- Crespelle

GOES WELL ON:
- Boiled potatoes
- Cooked meats (cold)
- Eggs
- Gnocchi
- Lasagna and cannelloni
- Pasta salad
- Polenta
- Raw meats and fish: tartare and carpaccio
- Rice and risotto
- Stuffed pasta (cheese, meat, or vegetables)

FRIED EGG SAUCE

Yield: 6 to 8 servings

6 eggs

1 bunch fresh chives, finely chopped

2 tablespoons (16 g) Soffrito (page 11)

2 cups (230 g) cubed string cheese

1 cup (100 g) grated grana (such as Asiago, Parmigiano-Reggiano, or Pecorino Romano)

Freshly grated nutmeg for seasoning

Salt and fresh-cracked black pepper

Olive oil

½ cup (120 ml) heavy cream

1 cup (100 g) stracchino cheese

½ pint (341 g) cherry tomatoes, finely chopped

1. In a large bowl, whisk the eggs. Add the chives, soffrito, string cheese, and grana. Season with a pinch of nutmeg and salt and pepper to taste. Whisk again to combine.

2. Brush a large skillet with a little oil and pour in the beaten egg mixture. Cook over medium heat while stirring gently until creamy and slightly set.

3. Stir in the cream and stracchino cheese and finish cooking to your desired doneness. Garnish with cherry tomatoes.

BEST ON:
- Bruschetta and crostini

GOES WELL ON:
- Cooked vegetables
- Pasta salad
- Pizza, focaccia, piadina
- Rice and risotto
- Rice salad

HARD-BOILED EGG SAUCE

Yield: 4 servings

2 salt-packed anchovies

6 hard-boiled eggs

1 tablespoon (9 g) brined
capers, drained and
chopped

Olive oil

Salt and fresh-cracked
black pepper

BEST ON:
- Al dente pasta
- Cooked meats or fish
  (hot or cold)
- Cooked vegetables

GOES WELL ON:
- Bruschetta and crostini
- Pasta salad
- Rice salad

1. Remove any bones, heads, and tails from the anchovies and rinse them under running water. Chop and set aside.

2. Peel the eggs, halve them, and scoop the yolks into a fine-mesh sieve set over a bowl. With the back of a spoon, push the egg yolks through the sieve. Transfer the egg yolks to a food processor or blender, or use an immersion blender. Slowing pouring in the oil (this may take up to 1 cup, or 240 ml, or more), blend until you have a smooth, creamy sauce. Transfer the sauce to a bowl.

3. Chop the egg whites very finely and add them to the sauce, along with the capers and anchovies. Whisk vigorously to combine.

4. Taste and season with salt and pepper.

5

ALL KINDS OF RAGÙS

RAGÙ OF BAKED ONIONS

Yield: 4 servings

4 large red onions

Coarse salt

¼ cup (33 g) Soffrito
  (page 11)

Olive oil

Salt and fresh-cracked
  black pepper

BEST ON:
- Boiled potatoes
- Cooked meats and fish
  (hot)
- Lasagna and cannelloni

GOES WELL ON:
- Bruschetta and crostini
- Cooked vegetables
- Crespelle
- Eggs
- Pizza, focaccia, piadina
- Veloutés and cream soups

1. Preheat the oven to 350°F (180°C, or gas mark 4).

2. Trim the onions without peeling them. Sprinkle a baking sheet with coarse salt, place the onions on it, and bake for 30 minutes.

3. Lower the oven temperature to 300°F (150°C, or gas mark 2) and bake the onions until tender (cook time will vary based on the size of the onions you use).

4. Remove the onions from the oven. When cool enough to handle, peel and chop them. Transfer the onions to a medium-size bowl and stir in the soffrito and a few swirls of oil.

5. Taste and season with salt and pepper.

CAULIFLOWER RAGÙ

1. Pour a few swirls of oil into a large skillet and add the cauliflower, onion, and chile. Cook over medium heat for 5 to 8 minutes until the vegetables begin to soften and brown.

2. Stir in the pine nuts, raisins, and soffrito. Pour in the water and cook, uncovered, for about 15 minutes until the cauliflower is tender and the sauce is thickened, adding more water if the sauce becomes dry, and stirring occasionally.

3. Taste and season with salt and pepper.

Yield: 4 to 6 servings

Olive oil

1 (about 2-pound, or 908 g) head cauliflower, coarsely chopped into florets

1 white onion, finely chopped

1 fresh chile pepper (such as serrano or jalapeño), destemmed, seeded and diced

¼ cup (34 g) pine nuts

¼ cup (35 g) raisins

¼ cup (33 g) Soffrito (page 11)

2 cups (480 ml) water, plus more as needed

Salt and fresh-cracked black pepper

BEST ON:
- Cooked pasta (all types)
- Stuffed pasta (cheese, meat, seafood, or vegetables)

GOES WELL ON:
- Cooked meats and fish (hot or cold)
- Cooked vegetables
- Raw meats and fish: tartare and carpaccio
- Stewed legumes
- Veloutés and cream soups

RED MUSHROOM RAGÙ

Yield: 4 servings

Olive oil

1 leek, trimmed and chopped

1 pound (454 g) mixed fresh
   mushrooms (such as
   cremini, oyster, porcini,
   white button), trimmed
   and diced

1½ cups (375 g) tomato purée

2 tablespoons (16 g)
   Soffrito (page 11)

Salt and fresh-cracked
   black pepper

1 bunch fresh parsley,
   chopped

1. Pour a few swirls of oil in a large skillet and add the leek. Sauté over medium heat for 4 to 5 minutes until the leek softens and begins to brown.

2. Add the mushrooms in a single layer, turn the heat to low, and cook for 5 minutes.

3. Stir in the tomato purée and soffrito, and cook over low heat for about 20 minutes, stirring occasionally, until the sauces reduces a bit and thickens.

4. Taste and season with salt and pepper, then sprinkle with the chopped parsley.

BEST ON:
- Al dente pasta
- Rice and risotto

GOES WELL ON:
- Boiled potatoes
- Cooked meats or fish
  (hot or cold)
- Crespelle
- Gnocchi
- Pasta salad
- Pizza, focaccia, piadina
- Polenta
- Raw meats and fish:
  tartare and carpaccio
- Stuffed pasta (cheese, meat,
  seafood, or vegetables)
- Veloutés and cream soups

ROMANESCO RAGÙ

Yield: 6 to 8 servings

Olive oil

1 white onion, finely chopped

1 fresh chile pepper (such
as serrano or jalapeño),
destemmed, seeded and
diced

About 5 ounces (140 g)
pancetta or bacon, diced

¼ cup (33 g) Soffrito
(page 11)

1 (about 2-pound, or 908 g)
head Romanesco
(Roman cauliflower),
finely chopped into florets

1 cup (240 ml) water,
plus more as needed

Salt and fresh-cracked
black pepper

1. Pour a few swirls of oil into a nonstick skillet and add the onion and chile. Sauté over medium heat for 3 to 5 minutes until softened and beginning to brown.

2. Add the pancetta and sauté for 2 minutes.

3. Stir in the soffrito and Romanesco, pour in the water, and cook for about 15 minutes until the Romanesco is soft and the sauce comes together, adding more water if the sauce becomes dry.

4. Taste and season with salt and pepper.

BEST ON:
- Al dente pasta
- Rice and risotto
- Stuffed pasta (cheese,
  meat, seafood, or vegetables)

GOES WELL ON:
- Cooked meats and fish
  (hot or cold)
- Cooked vegetables
- Crustaceans
- Raw meats and fish:
  tartare and carpaccio

RAGÙ OF CAVOLO BROCCOLO AND CHESTNUTS

Yield: 6 to 8 servings

1. Using the tip of a sharp knife, score the chestnuts with an X on the bottom.

2. Bring a large pot of salted water to a boil, add the chestnuts, and cook for about 40 minutes until the chestnuts are soft. Drain the chestnuts, let cool slightly, then remove them from their shells and skins. Coarsely chop the nuts.

3. Pour a few swirls of oil into nonstick skillet and add the onion and chile. Sauté over medium heat for 3 to 5 minutes until softened and beginning to brown.

4. Add the diced pancetta and cook for 3 to 4 minutes until it begins to render its fat and crisp around the edges.

5. Add the sprouting broccoli, soffrito, and chopped chestnuts. Pour in the water and cook for about 15 minutes until the sprouting broccoli is soft and the sauce comes together, adding more water if the sauce becomes dry.

6. Taste and season with salt and white pepper.

12 ounces (340 g) chestnuts

Salt and ground white pepper

Olive oil

1 white onion, finely chopped

1 fresh chile pepper (such as serrano or jalapeño), destemmed, seeded and diced

About 5 ounces (140 g) pancetta or bacon, diced

1 (about 2-pound, or 908 g) head cavolo broccolo (sprouting broccoli) or Chinese broccoli, coarsely chopped

2 tablespoons (16 g) Soffrito (page 11)

1 cup (240 ml) water, plus more as needed

BEST ON:
- Bruschetta and crostini
- Cooked pasta (any type)

GOES WELL ON:
- Cooked meats and fish (hot or cold)
- Cooked vegetables
- Crustaceans
- Pizza, focaccia, piadina
- Raw meats and fish: tartare and carpaccio
- Rice and risotto
- Veloutés and cream soups

WHITE VEGETABLE RAGÙ

Yield: 8 to 10 servings

Olive oil

1 pound (454 g) celery, diced

1 pound (454 g) carrots, diced

8 ounces (225 g) zucchini, diced

8 ounces (225 g) yellow bell pepper, diced

4 ounces (115 g) red onions, diced

4 ounces (115 g) white onions, diced

2 garlic cloves, peeled

1 bunch fresh parsley, chopped

¼ cup (33 g) Soffrito (page 11)

¾ cup (180 ml) vegetable broth for cooking

Salt and fresh-cracked black pepper

1. Pour a few generous swirls of oil into a large skillet and add the diced vegetables, half of the parsley, and garlic. Sauté over medium heat for about 5 minutes until the vegetables begin to soften and brown. The vegetables should be "al dente," so be careful not to overcook them.

2. Stir in the soffrito.

3. Adding broth a ladleful at a time, cook until much of the broth is absorbed by the vegetables, the vegetables are softened but still al dente, and the sauce is thick and luscious.

4. Taste and season with salt and pepper, then sprinkle with the remaining chopped parsley.

BEST ON:
- Cooked pasta (all types)
- Lasagna and cannelloni
- Stuffed pasta (cheese, meat, seafood, or vegetables)

GOES WELL ON:
- Cooked meats and fish (hot)
- Crespelle
- Crustaceans
- Gnocchi
- Pasta salad
- Polenta
- Rice and risotto
- Rice salad
- Veloutés and cream soups

RED VEGETABLE RAGÙ

1. Pour a few generous swirls of oil into a large skillet and add the diced vegetables and half of the parsley. Sauté over medium heat for about 5 minutes until the vegetables begin to soften and brown. The vegetables should be "al dente," so be careful not to overcook them.

2. Stir in the tomatoes and soffrito.

3. Adding broth a ladleful at a time, cook until much of the broth is absorbed by the vegetables, the vegetables are softened but still al dente, and the sauce is thick and luscious.

4. Taste and season with salt and pepper, then sprinkle with the remaining chopped parsley.

Yield: 8 to 10 servings

Olive oil

1 pound (454 g) celery, diced

1 pound (454 g) carrots, diced

8 ounces (225 g) zucchini, diced

8 ounces (225 g) red bell pepper, diced

8 ounces (225 g) cauliflower florets, diced

4 ounces (115 g) red onions, diced

4 ounces (115 g) white onions, diced

2 garlic cloves, peeled and diced

1 bunch fresh parsley, chopped

1 pound (454 g) cherry tomatoes, finely chopped

2 tablespoons (16 g) Soffrito (page 11)

¾ cup (180 ml) vegetable broth for cooking

Salt and fresh-cracked black pepper

BEST ON:
- Cooked pasta (all types)
- Lasagna and cannelloni
- Stuffed pasta (cheese, meat, seafood, or vegetables)

GOES WELL ON:
- Cooked meats and fish (hot)
- Cooked vegetables
- Crespelle
- Crustaceans

- Gnocchi
- Polenta
- Rice and risotto
- Veloutés and cream soups

SCOTTIGLIA RAGÙ

Yield: 6 to 8 servings

Olive oil

2 large carrots, finely chopped

1 red onion, finely chopped

1 celery stalk, finely chopped

1 bunch fresh parsley, finely
chopped

2 fresh chile peppers (such
as serrano or jalapeño),
destemmed, seeded and
finely chopped

3 pounds (1.3 kg) mixed meats
(such as beef, chicken, pork,
veal), diced

½ cup (120 ml) red wine

1 tablespoon (15 g) tomato paste

½ cup (120 ml) water

½ cup (120 ml) beef stock

¼ cup (33 g) Soffrito
(page 11)

Salt and fresh-cracked
black pepper

1. Pour a few generous swirls of oil into a large saucepan and add
the carrots, onion, celery, parsley, and chiles. Sauté over medium
heat for about 5 minutes until softened and beginning to brown.

2. Add the meats, turn the heat to high, and let cook for
10 minutes to brown, stirring occasionally.

3. Pour in the wine to deglaze the pan, scraping up any browned
bits from the bottom. Simmer for about 3 minutes until the
wine evaporates.

4. Meanwhile, in a small bowl, stir together the tomato paste and
water until the tomato paste dissolves. Add it to pan, along with
the stock and soffrito. Cover the pan and cook for 3 hours until
you have a thick sauce, stirring occasionally, and adding a little
water if the sauce becomes dry.

5. Taste and season with salt and pepper.

BEST ON:
- Cooked pasta (all types,
especially egg pasta)
- Gnocchi
- Polenta

GOES WELL ON:
- Boiled potatoes
- Bruschetta and crostini
- Crespelle
- Eggs
- Lasagna and cannelloni
- Pizza, focaccia, piadina
- Rice and risotto
- Stewed legumes
- Stuffed pasta (cheese,
meat, or vegetables)
- Veloutés and cream soups

RICH RAGÙ OF VEGETABLES AND PROVOLA CHEESE

1. Pour a few generous swirls of oil into a large skillet and add the diced vegetables and parsley. Sauté over medium heat for about 5 minutes until the vegetables begin to soften and brown. The vegetables should be "al dente," so be careful not to overcook them.

2. Stir in the soffrito.

3. Adding broth a ladleful at a time, cook until the broth is mostly absorbed, the vegetables are softened, but still al dente, and the sauce is thick and luscious.

4. Taste and season with salt and pepper.

5. Scatter the provola over the sauce, then stir to incorporate it into the sauce.

Yield: 8 to 10 servings

Olive oil

1 pound (454 g) celery, diced

1 pound (454 g) carrots, diced

8 ounces (225 g) cherry tomatoes, diced

8 ounces (225 g) zucchini, diced

4 ounces (115 g) red onions, diced

4 ounces (115 g) white onions, diced

⅔ cup (100 g) sliced green bell pepper, diced

⅔ cup (100 g) sliced red bell pepper, diced

⅔ cup (100 g) sliced yellow bell pepper, diced

2 garlic cloves, peeled and diced

1 bunch fresh parsley, chopped

2 tablespoons (16 g) Soffrito (page 11)

¾ cup (180 ml) vegetable broth

Salt and fresh-cracked black pepper

About 10 ounces (280 g) smoked provola cheese, chopped

BEST ON:
- Al dente pasta
- Lasagna and cannelloni

GOES WELL ON:
- Boiled potatoes
- Eggs
- Gnocchi
- Pasta salad
- Polenta
- Rice and risotto
- Veloutés and cream soups

GORGONZOLA OMELET RAGÙ

Yield: 4 to 6 servings

6 eggs

1 bunch fresh chives, finely chopped

8 ounces (225 g) Gorgonzola cheese, diced

4 ounces (115 g) grated grana (such as Asiago, Parmigiano-Reggiano, or Pecorino Romano)

Freshly grated nutmeg for seasoning

Salt and fresh-cracked black pepper

Olive oil

½ cup (120 ml) heavy cream

1. In a large bowl, whisk the eggs until blended. Add the chives, Gorgonzola, and grana. Season with a pinch of nutmeg and salt and pepper to taste and whisk to combine.

2. Pour a few swirls of oil into a skillet, tilting the pan to coat the bottom. Pour in the beaten egg mixture and cook over medium heat until the eggs are set. Gently flip the omelet and cook until the other side is set. Remove from the pan, let cool, and cut the omelet into strips.

3. In a saucepan, combine the cream and omelet strips. Cook over high heat for 4 minutes, stirring frequently, to reduce and thicken the sauce.

4. Taste and season with salt and pepper.

BEST ON:
- Boiled potatoes
- Cooked pasta (all types)
- Cooked vegetables
- Eggs

GOES WELL ON:
- Cooked meats (cold)

- Crespelle
- Gnocchi
- Lasagna and cannelloni
- Polenta
- Raw meats and fish: tartare and carpaccio
- Stuffed pasta (cheese, meat, or vegetables)

CHICKPEA AND SAUSAGE RAGÙ

1. Pour a few swirls of oil into a saucepan and add the garlic. Sauté over medium heat for about 1 minute until golden and fragrant.

2. Add the sausage and cook for 4 minutes, or until browned, stirring occasionally.

3. Stir in the chickpeas, soffrito, and 1 cup (240 ml) water. Increase the heat to medium-high and sauté for about 10 minutes until the chickpeas are tender and the sauce has thickened a little.

4. Taste and season with salt and pepper, then sprinkle on plenty of chopped parsley.

Yield: 4 servings

Olive oil

2 garlic cloves, peeled and finely chopped

About 10 ounces (280 g) Italian sausage, finely chopped

About 10 ounces (280 g) cooked or canned chickpeas, coarsely chopped

¼ cup (33 g) Soffrito (page 11)

1 cup (240 ml) water, plus more as needed

Salt and fresh-cracked black pepper

1 bunch fresh parsley, chopped

BEST ON:
- Gnocchi
- Stuffed pasta (cheese, meat, seafood, or vegetables)

GOES WELL ON:
- Bruschetta and crostini
- Cooked pasta (all types)
- Lasagna and cannelloni
- Polenta
- Rice and risotto

SALMON RAGÙ

Yield: 6 to 8 servings

1 celery stalk, finely chopped

1 large carrot, finely chopped

2 garlic cloves, peeled and finely chopped

1 bunch fresh parsley, finely chopped

Olive oil

1½ pounds (681 g) salmon fillets

½ cup (120 ml) rosé wine

1 tablespoon (15 g) tomato paste

1 cup (240 ml) fish stock

1½ cups (360 ml) cream

Himalayan pink salt and fresh-cracked pink peppercorns

1. Add the celery, carrot, garlic, and parsley to a saucepan. Pour in a few swirls of oil and cook over medium-low heat, stirring occasionally, for about 10 minutes until the vegetables are softened and browned.

2. Meanwhile, remove the skin and any bones from the salmon and finely chop it. Add the salmon to the pan, turn the heat to high, and sauté for 2 minutes.

3. Pour in the wine to deglaze the pan, scraping any browned bits from the bottom. Simmer for about 3 minutes until the wine evaporates.

4. In a small bowl, stir together the tomato paste and stock until the tomato paste dissolves, then add this to the pan, along with the cream. Turn the heat to low and cook for 5 minutes, or until warmed through.

5. Taste and season with salt and pepper.

BEST ON:
- Cooked pasta (all types)
- Rice and risotto

GOES WELL ON:
- Cooked fish (hot)
- Crespelle
- Crustaceans
- Gnocchi
- Lasagna and cannelloni
- Polenta
- Stuffed pasta (cheese, seafood, or vegetables)

WHITE FISH RAGÙ

1. Remove the skin and any bones from the fillets and cut the fish into small pieces.

2. Pour a few swirls of oil into a skillet and add the celery and carrot. Sauté over medium heat for 2 to 3 minutes until the vegetables soften and begin to brown. Stir in the garlic and sauté for about 30 seconds until fragrant.

3. Stir in the fish, cream, and soffrito. Simmer for about 6 to 8 minutes, or until the fish is just cooked through and flakes easily with a fork.

4. Taste and season with salt and pepper, then stir in the parsley.

Yield: 4 servings

1 pound (454 g) white sea bass, red snapper, or grouper fillets

Olive oil

1 celery stalk, finely chopped

1 large carrot, finely chopped

1 garlic clove, peeled and finely chopped

½ cup (120 ml) heavy cream

2 tablespoons (16 g) Soffrito (page 11)

Salt and fresh-cracked black pepper

1 bunch fresh parsley, chopped

BEST ON:
- Cooked fish (hot)
- Cooked pasta (all types)
- Stuffed pasta (cheese, seafood, or vegetables)

GOES WELL ON:
- Crespelle
- Crustaceans
- Gnocchi
- Rice and risotto
- Stewed legumes
- Veloutés and cream soups

SHRIMP AND PORCINI RAGÙ

Yield: 6 to 8 servings

Olive oil

1½ tablespoons (21 g) butter

1 garlic clove, unpeeled

1 fresh chile pepper (such as serrano or jalapeño), destemmed, seeded and diced

About 10 ounces (280 g) fresh porcini mushrooms, trimmed and cut into small pieces

½ cup (120 ml) white wine

¼ cup (33 g) Soffrito (page 11)

2 pounds (908 g) jumbo shrimp or langoustines, peeled, deveined, and chopped

1 bunch fresh parsley, chopped

Salt and fresh-cracked black pepper

1. In a skillet over medium heat, combine a few swirls of oil and the butter. When the butter melts, add the unpeeled garlic clove and chile. Sauté for 2 to 3 minutes until softened and beginning to brown. Crush the garlic with a wooden spoon, stir it into the oil to flavor it, then remove and discard the garlic.

2. Add the mushrooms, turn the heat to high, and cook for 10 minutes, stirring frequently, until browned.

3. Pour in the wine to deglaze the pan, scraping up any browned bits from the bottom. Stir in the soffrito. Turn the heat to medium and simmer for about 3 minutes until the wine evaporates.

4. Add the shrimp to the skillet and sauté for about 4 minutes until pink and opaque.

5. Add the parsley to the ragù.

6. Taste and season with salt and pepper.

BEST ON:
- Cooked pasta (all types)
- Gnocchi

GOES WELL ON:
- Bruschetta and crostini
- Cooked fish (hot)
- Crespelle
- Crustaceans
- Rice and risotto
- Stuffed pasta (cheese, seafood, or vegetables)
- Veloutés and cream soups

WHITE SARDINE RAGÙ

Yield: 4 servings

1 white celery stalk,
  finely chopped

1 large carrot, finely chopped

1 garlic clove, peeled,
  finely chopped

Olive oil

1 pound (454 g) fresh sardine
  fillets, chopped

½ cup (120 ml) heavy cream

Salt and fresh-cracked
  black pepper

1 bunch fresh parsley,
  chopped

BEST ON:
- Cooked pasta (all types)

GOES WELL ON:
- Bruschetta and crostini
- Gnocchi
- Pizza, focaccia, piadina
- Polenta
- Lasagna and cannelloni
- Stuffed pasta (cheese,
  seafood, or vegetables)

1. Add the celery, carrot, and garlic to a saucepan. Pour in a few swirls of oil and sauté over medium heat for 2 to 3 minutes until the vegetables begin to soften and brown.

2. Add the sardines to the pan. Cook for about 2 minutes, stirring, or until cooked through.

3. Pour in the cream and cook for 1 minute to heat through, stirring.

4. Taste and season with salt and pepper.

5. Stir the parsley into the sauce.

RED RAGÙ OF SHRIMP

1. Add the vegetables and half of the parsley to a saucepan and pour in a few swirls of oil. Cook, stirring occasionally, over medium-low heat for 10 minutes until softened and the onion is translucent.

2. Add the shrimp and turn the heat to high. Sauté for 2 minutes until the shrimp begin to turn pink.

3. Pour in the tomato sauce, scraping any browned bits from the bottom of the pan, and stir in the soffrito. Turn the heat to low and cook for about 2 minutes, or until the shrimp are cooked through and the sauce is warm.

4. Season with salt and pepper, then garnish with the remaining chopped parsley.

Yield: 4 servings

1 celery stalk, finely diced

1 carrot, finely diced

1 garlic clove, peeled and finely diced

1 bunch fresh parsley, finely diced

Olive oil

1 pound (454 g) jumbo shrimp or langoustines, peeled, deveined, and cut into chunks

½ cup (123 g) Tomato Sauce (page 98), or store-bought

¼ cup (33 g) Soffrito (page 11)

Salt and fresh-cracked black pepper

BEST ON:
- Cooked pasta (all types)
- Stuffed pasta (cheese, seafood, or vegetables)

GOES WELL ON:
- Boiled potatoes
- Cooked fish (hot)
- Crespelle
- Crustaceans
- Gnocchi
- Polenta
- Rice and risotto
- Veloutés and cream soups

WHITE RAGÙ OF RAZOR CLAMS

Yield: 4 servings

1 garlic clove, peeled

1 bunch fresh parsley

Olive oil

1 pound (454 g) razor clam meat, rinsed of any sand and finely chopped

½ cup (120 ml) white wine

1 tablespoon (15 g) tomato paste

½ cup (120 ml) water

¼ cup (33 g) Soffrito (page 11)

Salt and fresh-cracked black pepper

1. Chop together the garlic and parsley and transfer the chopped mixture to a skillet. Pour in a few swirls of oil and sauté over medium heat for about 30 seconds until fragrant.

2. Add the clam meat to the skillet.

3. Pour in the wine to deglaze the skillet, scraping up any browned bits from the bottom. Stir in the soffrito.

4. In a small bowl, stir together the tomato paste and water until the tomato paste dissolves, then add the mixture to the skillet. Stir to combine. Turn the heat to low and simmer for about 5 minutes until the clams are cooked through and the sauce is slightly thickened.

5. Taste and season with salt and pepper.

BEST ON:
- Bruschetta and crostini
- Cooked pasta (any type)
- Rice and risotto

GOES WELL ON:
- Boiled potatoes
- Bruschetta and crostini
- Cooked fish (hot)
- Crustaceans
- Gnocchi
- Pizza, focaccia, piadina
- Stuffed pasta (cheese, seafood, or vegetables)
- Veloutés and cream soups

RED RAGÙ OF RAZOR CLAMS

Yield: 4 servings

1. Chop the garlic and parsley together, transfer them to a skillet, and pour in a few swirls of oil. Sauté over medium heat for about 30 seconds until fragrant.

2. Stir in the tomatoes and cook for 2 minutes.

3. Add the clams to the skillet and pour in the wine to deglaze the pan, scraping up any browned bits from the bottom. Turn the heat to low and simmer for about 5 minutes until the wine evaporates and the clams are cooked through.

4. Taste and season with salt and pepper.

1 garlic clove, peeled

1 bunch fresh parsley

Olive oil

8 ounces (225 g) cherry tomatoes, roughly chopped

1 pound (454 g) razor clam meat, rinsed of any sand and finely chopped

½ cup (120 ml) white wine

Salt and fresh-cracked black pepper

BEST ON:
- Bruschetta and crostini
- Cooked pasta (any type)
- Rice and risotto

GOES WELL ON:
- Cooked fish (hot)
- Crespelle
- Crustaceans
- Gnocchi
- Pizza, focaccia, piadina
- Polenta
- Veloutés and cream soups

LOBSTER RAGÙ

Yield: 4 to 6 servings

Olive oil

1 fresh chile pepper (such as serrano or jalapeño), destemmed, seeded and diced

1 garlic clove, peeled and finely chopped

8 ounces (225 g) Tomato Sauce (page 98), or store-bought

1 cup (240 ml) fish stock, homemade or store-bought

¼ cup (33 g) Soffrito (page 11)

1 (about 2-pound, or 908 g) cooked lobster meat, deveined and cut into chunks

1 bunch fresh parsley, chopped

Salt and fresh-cracked black pepper

1. Pour a few swirls of oil into a saucepan and add the chile. Sauté over medium heat for about 2 minutes until the chile softens and begins to brown. Add the garlic and sauté for about 30 seconds until fragrant.

2. Stir in the tomato sauce, stock, and soffrito. Turn the heat to low and cook, uncovered, for 20 minutes.

3. Add the lobster meat and cook for 2 to 3 minutes until heated through.

4. Stir the parsley into the sauce.

5. Taste and season with salt and pepper.

BEST ON:
- Cooked pasta (all types)
- Rice and risotto

GOES WELL ON:
- Cooked fish (hot)
- Crustaceans
- Eggs
- Gnocchi
- Lasagna and cannelloni
- Polenta
- Stewed legumes
- Stuffed pasta (cheese, seafood, or vegetables)

CHICKEN RAGÙ

1. Add the vegetables to a large skillet.

2. Pour in a few swirls of oil and sauté over medium heat for 3 to 4 minutes until the vegetables begin to soften.

3. Add the chicken, and a bit more oil if the skillet is dry, and cook for 5 minutes, stirring occasionally, until browned.

4. Pour in the wine into the pan, scraping up any browned bits from the bottom. Simmer for about 3 minutes until the wine evaporates.

5. Stir in the soffrito, add the rosemary, and cover the skillet. Turn the heat to low and cook for 20 to 25 minutes, adding a little water if the sauce becomes dry, until the chicken is cooked through (no pink remains) and the sauce is thickened. Remove and discard the rosemary.

6. Taste and season with salt and pepper.

Yield: 4 servings

1 white onion, chopped

1 celery stalk, chopped

1 large carrot, chopped

Olive oil

1 pound (454 g) boneless, skinless chicken thighs, chopped into bite-size pieces

½ cup (120 ml) white wine

¼ cup (33 g) Soffrito (page 11)

1 rosemary sprig

Salt and fresh-cracked black pepper

BEST ON:
- Cooked pasta (all types, especially egg pasta)
- Rice and risotto

GOES WELL ON:
- Bruschetta and crostini
- Crespelle
- Gnocchi
- Lasagna and cannelloni
- Pizza, focaccia, piadina
- Polenta
- Stuffed pasta (cheese or vegetables)

FARMER'S CHICKEN AND SAUSAGE RAGÙ

Yield: 4 to 6 servings

1 leek, trimmed and finely chopped

1 celery stalk, finely chopped

1 large carrot, finely chopped

Olive oil

1 pound (454 g) ground chicken

4 ounces (115 g) sweet Italian sausage, finely chopped

¼ cup (60 ml) grappa or chicken broth

1 bunch fresh parsley, chopped

2 tablespoons (16 g) Soffrito (page 11)

¼ cup (25 g) pitted black olives

Salt and fresh-cracked black pepper

1. Transfer the vegetables to a saucepan and pour in a few swirls of oil. Sauté over medium heat for 3 to 5 minutes until the vegetables soften and begin to brown.

2. Add the ground chicken and sausage. Turn the heat to high and sauté the meats, breaking them up with the back of a wooden spoon, for 3 to 5 minutes until golden brown.

3. Pour in the grappa to deglaze the pan, scraping up any browned bits from the bottom. Cook for about 3 minutes until the grappa evaporates.

4. Add the parsley to the pan. Stir in the soffrito and olives, turn the heat to medium-low, and cook for 20 minutes until the chicken and sausage are cooked through (no pink remains) and the sauce is thickened, adding a little water if the sauce becomes dry.

5. Taste and season with salt and pepper.

BEST ON:
- Cooked pasta (all types, especially egg pasta)
- Stuffed pasta (cheese, meat, or vegetables)

GOES WELL ON:
- Boiled potatoes
- Bruschetta and crostini
- Eggs
- Gnocchi
- Lasagna and cannelloni
- Polenta

TURKEY RAGÙ WITH YELLOW PEPPERS

Yield: 6 servings

8 ounces (225 g) yellow
    bell peppers, sliced

1 red onion, diced

1 celery stalk, diced

1 large carrot, diced

1 bunch fresh parsley, chopped

Olive oil

1½ pounds (681 g) ground
    turkey

½ cup (120 ml) dry white wine

Vegetable broth for cooking

2 tablespoons (16 g)
    Soffrito (page 11)

Salt and fresh-cracked
    black pepper

BEST ON:
- Cooked pasta (all types,
  especially egg pasta)
- Lasagna and cannelloni

GOES WELL ON:
- Boiled potatoes
- Gnocchi
- Rice and risotto
- Stuffed pasta (cheese,
  meat, or vegetables)

1. Bring a saucepan full of water to a boil, add the bell pepper slices, and blanch for 2 minutes. Drain the peppers, reserving ½ cup (120 ml) of the blanching water. Transfer half of the peppers to a food processor or blender and blend until smooth, adding just enough of the reserved blanching water, a little at a time, to achieve a purée.

2. Add the onion, celery, and carrot to the empty saucepan. Add the parsley to the pan, along with a few generous swirls of oil. Sauté over medium heat for about 5 minutes until the vegetables soften and begin to brown.

3. Add the ground turkey, turn the heat to medium-high, and sauté for 5 minutes until no longer pink.

4. Pour in the wine to deglaze the pan, scraping up any browned bits from the bottom. Simmer for about 3 minutes until the wine evaporates.

5. Pour in enough broth to cover the ingredients in the pan and stir in the soffrito. Turn the heat to low and simmer for 50 minutes until the sauce thickens, stirring occasionally and adding more broth if the sauce becomes dry.

6. Stir in the puréed peppers and remaining blanched sliced peppers. Cook for 10 minutes to heat through.

7. Taste and season with salt and pepper.

DUCK RAGÙ

1. Add the vegetables to a saucepan along with a few swirls of oil and cook for 3 to 5 minutes over medium heat until the vegetables begin to soften and brown.

2. Finely chop the duck meat together with the livers and add them to the pan, along with the bay leaves and thyme. Cook, stirring occasionally, until the duck is golden brown.

3. Pour in the wine to deglaze the pan, scraping up any browned bits from the bottom. Simmer for about 3 minutes until the wine evaporates.

4. Stir in the soffrito and broth. Turn the heat to low, cover the pan tightly, and cook for 1 hour until the ragù is thick and the meat is tender.

5. Remove and discard the bay leaves and thyme.

6. Taste and season with salt and pepper.

Yield: 4 to 6 servings

1 red onion, finely chopped

1 celery stalk, finely chopped

1 carrot, finely chopped

Olive oil

12 ounces (340 g) duck meat

4 ounces (115 g) duck livers

2 bay leaves

1 bunch fresh thyme

½ cup (120 ml) red wine

¼ cup (33 g) Soffrito (page 11)

1¼ cups (300 ml) vegetable broth

Salt and fresh-cracked black pepper

BEST ON:
- Al dente pasta (especially egg pasta)

GOES WELL ON:
- Boiled potatoes
- Crespelle
- Eggs
- Gnocchi
- Lasagna and cannelloni
- Pizza, focaccia, piadina
- Polenta
- Stuffed pasta (cheese, meat, or vegetables)

CLASSIC RAGÙ

Yield: 4 servings

1 onion, diced

1 celery stalk, diced

1 carrot, diced

2 tablespoons (28 g) butter

1 tablespoon minced cured
   lard (fatback) or pancetta

About 5 ounces (140 g)
   ground pork

4 ounces (115 g) ground veal

4 ounces (115 g) ground
   chicken

¼ cup (60 ml) dry red wine

About 10 ounces (280 g)
   peeled whole tomatoes,
   fresh or canned

1 teaspoon tomato conserva
   or tomato paste

Salt and fresh-cracked
   black pepper

1. Add the onion, celery, and carrot to a large saucepan along
   with the butter and lard. Cook over medium-low heat for
   about 20 minutes, stirring occasionally, until the vegetables
   are very soft.

2. Add the ground pork, veal, and chicken. Turn the heat to
   medium and cook slowly, breaking up the meats with the back
   of a wooden spoon, for 10 to 15 minutes, or until browned and
   cooked through (no pink remains).

3. Pour in the wine to deglaze the pan, scraping up any browned
   bits from the bottom. Simmer for about 3 minutes until the
   wine evaporates.

4. Stir in the tomatoes and conserva. Turn the heat to low and
   simmer for 1 hour 20 minutes, stirring occasionally to break up
   the tomatoes, adding a bit of water if the sauce becomes dry.
   The sauce will be thick.

5. Taste and season with salt and pepper.

BEST ON:
- Cooked pasta (all types,
  especially egg pasta)
- Stuffed pasta (cheese,
  meat, or vegetables)

GOES WELL ON:
- Boiled potatoes
- Bruschetta and crostini
- Gnocchi
- Lasagna and cannelloni
- Polenta
- Stewed legumes

RICH AND MEATY RAGÙ

1. Add the pancetta and lard to a large saucepan. Pour in a few swirls of oil and sweat the lard and pancetta over medium-low heat for 5 to 7 minutes until they begin to render their fat and crisp up around the edges.

2. Add the sausage to the pan, along with the diced vegetables, parsley, and ground beef. Turn the heat to high and cook, stirring frequently and breaking up the meat with the back of a wooden spoon, for about 5 minutes until browned and the vegetables soften.

3. Pour in the wine to deglaze the pan, scraping up any browned bits from the bottom. Turn the heat to medium and simmer for about 3 minutes until the wine evaporates.

4. Add the cherry tomatoes and pour in the tomato purée. Cover the pan, turn the heat to low, and cook for 2 hours, stirring occasionally to prevent it from sticking to the bottom of the pan, and adding a little water if the sauce becomes dry.

5. Taste and season with salt and pepper.

Yield: 6 to 8 servings

4 ounces (115 g) pancetta or bacon, diced

1½ ounces (42 g) cured lard (fatback) or salt pork (which will be saltier), diced

Olive oil

12 ounces (340 g) sweet Italian sausage, cut into chunks

3 red onions, finely chopped

2 carrots, finely chopped

1 celery stalk, finely chopped

1 bunch fresh parsley, finely chopped

1 pound (454 g) ground beef

1 cup (240 ml) red wine

About 10 ounces (280 g) cherry tomatoes

4 cups (1 kg) tomato purée

Salt and fresh-cracked black pepper

BEST ON:
- Lasagna and cannelloni
- Stuffed pasta (cheese or vegetables)

GOES WELL ON:
- Cooked meats (hot)
- Cooked pasta (all types)
- Cooked vegetables
- Crespelle
- Gnocchi
- Pizza, focaccia, piadina
- Polenta

BERLIN-STYLE FRICASSEE RAGÙ

4 ounces (115 g) veal
   sweetbreads

4 tablespoons (½ stick,
   or 56 g) butter

4 ounces (115 g) champignon
   (white button)
   mushrooms, trimmed
   and chopped

1 onion, chopped

4 boneless, skinless chicken
   thighs, chopped

½ cup (120 ml) white wine

12 shrimp, peeled, deveined,
   and chopped

4 ounces (115 g) cooked veal
   tongue or beef tongue,
   diced

8 oil-packed anchovy fillets,
   or 4 teaspoons (18 g)
   anchovy paste

¼ cup (33 g) Soffrito
   (page 11)

Juice of ½ lemon, strained

1 handful brined capers,
   drained

Salt and fresh-cracked
   black pepper

2 large egg yolks

1. In a large bowl of cold water, soak the sweetbreads for 3 hours to remove any blood, changing the water frequently. Drain.

2. Bring a saucepan full of water to a boil, add the sweetbreads, and blanch for 30 seconds. Drain, let cool until they can be handled, then remove any fat and sinew, along with the membrane. Chop the sweetbreads.

3. In a skillet over medium heat, melt 2 tablespoons (28 g) of butter. Add the chopped sweetbreads and cook for about 5 minutes, stirring frequently, until browned. Transfer the sweetbreads to a bowl, leaving any melted butter behind in the skillet, and return the skillet to medium heat.

4. Add the mushrooms in a single layer and cook for about 4 minutes, stir, and cook for 3 to 5 minutes more until browned. Transfer to the bowl with the sweetbreads.

5. Return the skillet to medium heat and add the remaining 2 tablespoons (28 g) of butter to melt, then add the onion and chicken thighs. Cook for 5 minutes, stirring occasionally, until browned.

6. Pour in the wine to deglaze the skillet, scraping up any browned bits from the bottom. Add the sweetbreads and sautéed mushrooms, chopped shrimp, diced tongue, anchovies, and the soffrito to the skillet. Stir to combine and cook for about 3 minutes until the shrimp are pink and everything is heated through.

7. Stir in the lemon juice and capers. Taste and season with salt and pepper. Remove the skillet from the heat and gently stir in the egg yolks to bind the sauce.

BEST ON:
- Al dente pasta
  (especially egg pasta)
- Rice and risotto

GOES WELL ON:
- Cooked pasta (all types)
- Polenta

BRAISED BEEF RAGÙ WITH RED WINE

Yield: 4 to 6 servings

1. In a medium-size saucepan over medium-high heat, combine the wine and mushrooms. Bring to a boil and cook until the liquid is reduced by half. Drain, reserving the wine, and discard the mushrooms.

2. Return the saucepan to medium heat and add the butter to melt. Add the onion, celery, and carrot and sauté for 3 to 5 minutes until softened and beginning to brown.

3. Add the beef, increase the heat to high, and cook for about 5 minutes, stirring occasionally, until browned.

4. Add the sage and rosemary. Pour in the reserved wine and stir in the soffrito. Cover the pan and cook for about 1 hour until the meat is very tender, adding a little hot water if the sauce becomes dry. Remove and discard the sage and rosemary.

5. Taste and season with salt and pepper.

1½ cups (360 ml) full-bodied red wine

2 ounces (55 g) champignon (white button) mushrooms

3½ tablespoons (49 g) butter

1 red onion, diced

1 celery stalk, diced

1 large carrot, diced

1 pound (454 g) beef (preferably chuck), diced

1 bunch fresh sage

1 rosemary sprig

¼ cup (33 g) Soffrito (page 11)

Salt and fresh-cracked black pepper

BEST ON:
- Cooked pasta (all types)
- Polenta
- Rice and risotto

GOES WELL ON:
- Crespelle
- Boiled potatoes

- Eggs
- Gnocchi
- Lasagna and cannelloni
- Pizza, focaccia, piadina
- Stewed legumes
- Stuffed pasta (cheese, meat, or vegetables)
- Veloutés and cream soups

BEEF RAGÙ PIZZAIOLA STYLE

Yield: 6 to 8 servings

1 bunch fresh oregano, stems removed

1 red onion, diced

1 celery stalk, diced

1 large carrot, diced

1 bunch fresh parsley, chopped

Olive oil

1½ pounds (681 g) ground beef

4 cups (1 kg) tomato purée

Salt and fresh-cracked black pepper

1½ cups (175 g) diced mozzarella cheese

BEST ON:
- Cooked pasta (especially shells, penne, and other ridged pastas)
- Gnocchi

GOES WELL ON:
- Boiled potatoes
- Lasagna and cannelloni
- Polenta
- Stewed legumes
- Stuffed pasta (cheese or vegetables)

1. Remove the oregano leaves from the stems and discard the stems.

2. Add the vegetables and parsley to a saucepan. Pour in a few swirls of oil and sauté over medium heat for 3 to 5 minutes until the vegetables begin to soften and brown.

3. Add the ground beef, turn the heat to high, and sauté for 5 minutes until browned, breaking up the beef with the back of a wooden spoon.

4. Stir in the tomato purée and oregano. Turn the heat to low and simmer for 1 hour until fragrant and thickened, stirring often, and adding a little water if the sauce becomes dry.

5. Taste and season with salt and pepper.

6. Add the mozzarella and stir vigorously to incorporate and melt the cheese into the sauce.

7. Finish with a drizzle of oil.

NEAPOLITAN RAGÙ GENOVESE STYLE

1. Pour a few generous swirls of oil into a large pot and add the beef in a single piece. Cook over medium heat for about 8 minutes, turning, or until browned on all sides.

2. Pour in the wine to deglaze the pot, scraping up any browned bits from the bottom. Simmer for about 3 minutes until the wine evaporates.

3. Add the carrots, celery, parsley, onions, and soffrito to the pot.

4. In a small bowl, stir together the tomato paste and water until the tomato paste dissolves, add it to the pot, and stir to combine the ingredients. Add the salami to the pot.

5. Cover the pot, turn the heat to low, and cook for about 4 hours until the beef is very tender, stirring occasionally to make sure it's not sticking, and adding a little hot water if the sauce becomes dry.

6. Remove the meat, shred it, and return it to the pot, stirring to combine with the sauce.

7. Taste and season with and salt and pepper.

Yield: 4 to 6 servings

Olive oil

1 pound (454 g) boneless beef roast (such as chuck)

1 cup (240 ml) dry white wine

2 carrots, finely chopped

1 small celery stalk, finely chopped

1 bunch fresh parsley, finely chopped

1 pound (454 g) onions, chopped

¼ cup (33 g) Soffrito (page 11)

1 tablespoon (15 g) tomato paste

½ cup (120 ml) water

1 small piece salami, about 2 inches (5 cm) long, chopped

Salt and fresh-cracked black pepper

BEST ON:
- Al dente rigatoni (or other ridged pasta)

GOES WELL ON:
- Boiled potatoes
- Cooked pasta (all types)
- Crespelle
- Gnocchi
- Lasagna and cannelloni
- Pizza, focaccia, piadina
- Polenta
- Rice and risotto
- Stewed legumes
- Veloutés and cream soups

SAUSAGE RAGÙ

Yield: 6 to 8 servings

1 red onion, diced

1 celery stalk, diced

1 large carrot, diced

1 bunch fresh parsley

Olive oil

1½ pounds (681 g) sweet
   Italian sausage, chopped

½ cup (120 ml) white wine

½ cup (120 ml) milk

¼ cup (33 g) Soffrito
   (page 11)

Salt and fresh-cracked
   black pepper

BEST ON:
- Cooked pasta (all types,
  especially egg pasta)
- Polenta

GOES WELL ON:
- Boiled potatoes
- Eggs
- Gnocchi
- Lasagna and cannelloni
- Pizza, focaccia, piadina
- Polenta
- Stuffed pasta (cheese,
  meta, or vegetables)

1. Add the onion, celery, carrot, and parsley to a saucepan. Pour in a few swirls of oil. Sauté over medium heat for 3 to 5 minutes until the vegetables begin to soften and brown.

2. Add the sausage to the pan. Turn the heat to high and sauté for 5 minutes to brown the sausage.

3. Pour in the wine to deglaze the pan, scraping any browned bits from the bottom. Simmer for about 3 minutes until the wine evaporates.

4. Stir in the milk and soffrito. Turn the heat to low and simmer for 20 minutes until the sauce is thickened slightly.

5. Taste and season with salt and pepper.

OXTAIL RAGÙ

1. In a medium-size bowl, combine the raisins with enough hot water to cover and let soak for 20 minutes. Drain and squeeze the excess water from the raisins.

2. Meanwhile, in a small nonstick skillet over medium-high heat, toast the pine nuts for 2 to 3 minutes until lightly browned and fragrant. Set aside.

3. Pour a few swirls of oil into a large saucepan and add the oxtail. Sear over medium heat, turning, until browned all over.

4. Pour in the wine to deglaze the pan, scraping up any browned bits from the bottom.

5. Add the celery, onion, carrot, and parsley and stir in the tomato purée. Pour in enough water to cover the ingredients, turn the heat to low, and cook for about 2 hours until the meat and vegetables are tender, adding more hot water if the sauce becomes dry.

6. Remove the oxtail pieces, pull the meat from the bones, cut up the meat, and return the meat to the sauce. Discard the bones.

7. Stir in the chocolate, soaked raisins, and toasted pine nuts.

8. Taste and season with salt and pepper. Simmer the sauce for 5 minutes more to reduce and thicken.

Yield: 6 servings

1 handful raisins

1 handful pine nuts

Olive oil

2 pounds (908 g) oxtail, cut into pieces

½ cup (120 ml) red wine

4 celery stalks, minced

1 red onion, minced

1 carrot, minced

1 bunch fresh parsley, minced

1⅔ cups (333 g) tomato purée

2 tablespoons (16 g) grated bittersweet chocolate

Salt and fresh-cracked black pepper

BEST ON:
- Cooked pasta (all types)
- Gnocchi
- Stuffed pasta (cheese and vegetables)

GOES WELL ON:
- Boiled potatoes
- Bruschetta and crostini
- Pizza, focaccia, piadina
- Polenta
- Rice and risotto

RAGÙ OF OSSO BUCO

Yield: 4 servings

8 veal shanks (¾ inch,
    or 2 cm, thick)

All-purpose flour for dusting

3 tablespoons (42 g) butter

3 cups (720 ml) veal broth or
    vegetable broth, plus more
    as needed

1 tablespoon (15 g) tomato
    paste

½ cup (120 ml) water

6 tablespoons (85 g) Soffrito
    (page 11)

½ cup (120 ml) dry white wine

1 bunch fresh parsley,
    chopped

1 garlic clove, peeled
    and chopped

1 organic lemon

Salt and fresh-cracked
    black pepper

BEST ON:
- Bruschetta and crostini
- Cooked pasta
- Polenta
- Rice and risotto

1. Remove the meat from the bones, reserving the bones, and cut the meat into chunks. Dust the veal with flour, tossing it to coat.

2. In a saucepan over medium heat, melt the butter. Add the veal meat and bones and cook for about 5 minutes to brown.

3. In a small saucepan, bring the broth to a boil. Reduce the heat to maintain a simmer, adding more broth to keep warm as needed.

4. In a small bowl, stir together the tomato paste and water until the tomato paste dissolves. Stir the mixture into the pan with the veal, along with the soffrito.

5. Pour in the wine to deglaze the pan, scraping up any browned bits from the bottom. Simmer for about 3 minutes until the wine evaporates. Cover the pan, turn the heat to low, and cook for 1 hour, stirring and basting with a ladleful of hot broth occasionally as the sauce becomes dry.

6. Remove the pan from the heat and let cool. Shred the meat and remove the marrow from the bones. Return the shredded meat and marrow to the saucepan. Discard the bones. Place the pan over medium heat and cook for 10 minutes until the sauce is warmed through and thickened slightly.

7. Stir the parsley and garlic into the sauce. Grate the zest of ½ lemon over the sauce and stir to combine.

8. Taste and season with salt and pepper.

SKIRT STEAK RAGÙ

Yield: 4 servings

1 large white onion, finely
   chopped

Olive oil

1 pound (454 g) skirt steak,
   diced

½ cup (120 ml) dry white
   wine

¼ cup (33 g) Soffrito
   (page 11)

Salt and fresh-cracked
   black pepper

1 bunch fresh parsley,
   chopped

BEST ON:
- Al dente egg pasta

GOES WELL ON:
- Bruschetta and crostini
- Cooked pasta
- Crespelle
- Gnocchi
- Lasagna and cannelloni
- Rice and risotto
- Stewed legumes
- Stuffed pasta (meat,
  cheese, or vegetables)

1. Place the onion in a saucepan with a few swirls of oil. Sauté over medium heat for about 3 minutes until the onion begins to soften and brown.

2. Add the steak, increase the heat to high, and sauté for 5 minutes until browned.

3. Pour in the wine to deglaze the pan, scraping up any browned bits from the bottom. Simmer for about 3 minutes until the wine evaporates.

4. Stir in the soffrito.

5. Taste and season with salt and pepper, then sprinkle with plenty of chopped parsley.

RAGÙ OF FILET MIGNON WITH MONTALCINO RED WINE

Yield: 4 servings

1. Add the onion, celery, carrot, and rosemary leaves to a saucepan and pour in a few swirls of oil. Sauté over medium heat for about 5 minutes until the vegetables soften and begin to brown.

2. Add the filet mignon to the pan. Cook for about 2 minutes, stirring until it begins to brown.

3. Pour in the wine to glaze the pan, scraping up any browned bits from the bottom. Simmer for about 3 minutes until the wine evaporates.

4. In a small bowl, stir together the tomato paste and water until the tomato paste dissolves. Stir the mixture into the sauce, along with the soffrito. Turn the heat to low and cook for 5 minutes until the filet is cooked through and the sauce is warm.

5. Taste and season with salt and pepper.

1 white onion, finely diced

1 celery stalk, finely diced

1 large carrot, finely diced

1 rosemary sprig, finely diced

Olive oil

1 pound (454 g) filet mignon, diced

½ cup (120 ml) Rosso di Montalcino red wine or other dry, fruity red wine

1 tablespoon (15 g) tomato paste

½ cup (120 ml) water

¼ cup (33 g) Soffrito (page 11)

Salt and fresh-cracked black pepper

BEST ON:
- Al dente pasta (especially egg pasta)

GOES WELL ON:
- Boiled potatoes
- Bruschetta and crostini
- Cooked pasta (any type)
- Crespelle
- Gnocchi
- Lasagna and cannelloni
- Pizza, focaccia, piadina
- Polenta
- Rice and risotto
- Stewed legumes
- Stuffed pasta (cheese, meat, or vegetables)

MEATBALL RAGÙ

Yield: 6 to 8 servings

1 cup (50 g) torn soft bread
    pieces

Milk for soaking

4 cups (1 kg) tomato purée

1 pound (454 g) ground beef

2 garlic cloves, peeled
    and minced

1 egg

4 ounces (115 g) grated
    Pecorino Romano cheese

Salt and fresh-cracked
    black pepper

½ cup (60 g) breadcrumbs

Olive oil

2 tablespoons (16 g)
    Soffrito (page 11)

BEST ON:
- Cooked pasta (all types)
- Pizza, focaccia, piadina

GOES WELL ON:
- Bruschetta and crostini
- Gnocchi
- Lasagna and cannelloni
- Polenta
- Rice and risotto

1. In a small bowl, combine the bread pieces in enough milk to cover and let soak for a few minutes. Drain and squeeze the excess milk from the bread.

2. Pour the tomato purée into a saucepan and simmer over low heat for 15 minutes.

3. In a large bowl, combine the ground beef, garlic, egg, Pecorino Romano, and soaked bread. Season with salt and pepper and mix to combine. Form the mixture into very small (about 1 inch, or 2.5 cm) meatballs.

4. Place the breadcrumbs in a shallow bowl and roll the meatballs in the crumbs to coat.

5. Pour a few swirls of oil into a large skillet and add the meatballs. Sauté over medium heat for 5 minutes, stirring gently, to brown. Transfer the meatballs to the tomato purée, stir in the soffrito, and simmer over low heat for 5 minutes to thicken slightly.

6. Taste the sauce and season with salt and pepper.

NEAPOLITAN RAGÙ

1. In a medium bowl, stir together the tomato paste and hot water until the tomato paste dissolves.

2. Pour a few generous swirls of oil into a large saucepan and add the beef. Cook over medium-high heat, stirring frequently, for 5 minutes to brown.

3. Pour in the wine to deglaze the pan, scraping up any browned bits from the bottom. Simmer for about 3 minutes until the wine evaporates.

4. Pour in the tomato paste mixture.

5. Stir the pancetta into the sauce, along with the sautéed onions.

6. Add the basil to the sauce with the sugar. Stir to combine. Cover the pan, turn the heat to very low, and cook for 6 hours, adding a little hot water if the sauce becomes dry. Continue cooking the sauce, uncovered, until the sauce is thick, dark, and glossy.

7. Taste and season with salt and red pepper flakes.

Yield: 6 to 8 servings

4 cups (1 kg) tomato paste

4 cups (960 ml) hot water

Olive oil

2 pounds (908 g) beef chuck roast, chopped

½ cup (120 ml) full-bodied red wine

About 5 ounces (140 g) pancetta or prosciutto, coarsely chopped

½ cup (44 g) sautéed onions

1 bunch fresh basil, chopped

1 tablespoon (12.5 g) sugar

Salt

Red pepper flakes for seasoning

BEST ON:
- Cooked pasta (all types)

GOES WELL ON:
- Boiled potatoes
- Crespelle
- Gnocchi
- Lasagna and cannelloni
- Polenta
- Rice and risotto
- Stuffed pasta (cheese, meat, or vegetables)

RAGÙ OF PORK CHEEK WITH NEBBIOLO WINE

Yield: 4 servings

1 red onion, finely chopped

1 celery stalk, finely chopped

1 medium-size carrot, finely chopped

Olive oil

1 pound (454 g) pork cheek, diced

½ cup (120 ml) Nebbiolo wine

1 teaspoon dried marjoram for seasoning

1 tablespoon (15 g) tomato paste

½ cup (120 ml) water

¼ cup (33 g) Soffrito (page 11)

Salt and fresh-cracked black pepper

1. Add the onion, celery, and carrot to a saucepan. Pour in a few swirls of oil and sauté over medium heat for about 5 minutes until the vegetables soften and turn golden brown.

2. Add the pork cheek and cook for about 5 minutes to brown.

3. Pour in the wine to deglaze the pan, scraping up any browned bits from the bottom. Stir in the marjoram to taste.

4. In a small bowl, stir together the tomato paste and water until the tomato paste dissolves. Add it to the pan, along with the soffrito, and stir to combine. Turn the heat to low and cook for 1 hour until the pork is tender and the sauce has thickened, adding a little hot water if the sauce becomes dry.

5. Taste and season with salt and pepper.

BEST ON:
• Al dente egg pasta

GOES WELL ON:
• Boiled potatoes
• Crespelle
• Eggs
• Gnocchi
• Polenta
• Rice and risotto
• Stewed legumes

RAGÙ OF PORK CHEEK ALLA CACCIATORA

1. Add the onion, celery, and carrot to a saucepan. Pour in a few swirls of oil and sauté over medium heat for about 5 minutes until the vegetables soften and turn golden brown.

2. Add the pork cheek to the pan. Cook for about 5 minutes to brown.

3. Pour in the wine to deglaze the pan, scraping up any browned bits from the bottom.

4. Add the sausage to the pan, along with the soffrito, olives, rosemary, and bay leaves. Stir to combine. Cover the pan, turn the heat to low, and cook for 1 hour until the meat is tender, adding a little hot water if the sauce becomes dry. Remove and discard the rosemary and bay leaves.

5. Taste and season with salt and pepper.

Yield: 6 to 8 servings

1 red onion, chopped

1 celery stalk, chopped

1 large carrot, chopped

Olive oil

1 pound (454 g) pork cheek, diced

½ cup (120 ml) white wine

About 10 ounces (280 g) sweet Italian sausage, cut into small pieces

¼ cup (33 g) Soffrito (page 11)

¾ cup (75 g) pitted black olives

1 rosemary sprig

2 bay leaves

Salt and fresh-cracked black pepper

BEST ON:
- Al dente egg pasta

GOES WELL ON:
- Boiled potatoes
- Gnocchi
- Lasagna and cannelloni
- Polenta
- Rice and risotto

RED RAGÙ OF PORK CHOPS

Yield: 4 servings

1 handful raisins

Olive oil

1 large white onion, finely
    chopped

8 (about 4-ounce, or 115 g)
    thin-cut boneless pork chops,
    cut into bite-size pieces

4 ounces (115 g) ham, cut into
    bite-size pieces

2½ cups (625 g) tomato purée

¼ cup (33 g) Soffrito
    (page 11)

1 bunch fresh basil leaves,
    chopped with stems
    removed

1 bunch fresh parsley, chopped

Salt and fresh-cracked
    black pepper

1. In a medium-size bowl, combine the raisins with enough hot water to cover and let soak for 20 minutes. Drain and squeeze the excess water from the raisins.

2. Pour a few swirls of oil into a large saucepan, add the onion, and sauté over medium heat for about 5 minutes, or until golden brown.

3. Add the pork and ham, increase the heat to high, and cook for 5 minutes, stirring occasionally, until browned.

4. Pour in the tomato purée, add the soffrito, and bring to a boil. Cover the skillet with a lid, turn the heat to medium, and cook for 1 hour, adding hot water, a little at a time, if the sauce becomes dry.

5. Stir in the soaked raisins.

6. Stir the basil and parsley into the sauce.

7. Taste and season with salt and pepper.

BEST ON:
- Cooked pasta (all types)
- Lasagna and cannelloni

GOES WELL ON:
- Boiled potatoes
- Gnocchi
- Polenta
- Rice and risotto
- Stewed legumes
- Stuffed pasta (cheese, meat, or vegetables)

RED LAMB RAGÙ

1. Pour a few swirls of oil into a saucepan and add the onion, celery, carrot, and chile. Sauté over medium heat for 3 to 5 minutes, or until softened and lightly browned.

2. Add the lamb and let it cook for a few minutes undisturbed.

3. Pour in the wine to deglaze the pan, scraping up any browned bits from the bottom. Simmer for about 3 minutes until the wine evaporates.

4. Stir in the rosemary, tomatoes, soffrito, and a splash of water. Turn the heat to low and cook for 1 hour 30 minutes until the lamb is tender and the sauce is thickened, adding a little hot water if the sauce becomes dry.

5. Taste and season with salt and pepper.

Yield: 2 to 4 servings

Olive oil

1 red onion, diced

1 celery stalk, diced

1 medium-size carrot, diced

1 fresh chile pepper (such as serrano or jalapeño), destemmed, seeded and diced

8 ounces (225 g) lamb meat, cut into small pieces

½ cup (120 ml) white wine

1 rosemary sprig

8 ounces (225 g) cherry tomatoes, chopped

¼ cup (33 g) Soffrito (page 11)

Salt and fresh-cracked black pepper

BEST ON:
- Al dente pasta (especially egg pasta)
- Gnocchi
- Lasagna and cannelloni

GOES WELL ON:
- Boiled potatoes
- Bruschetta and crostini
- Cooked pasta (all types)
- Crespelle
- Eggs
- Pizza, focaccia, piadina
- Polenta
- Rice and risotto
- Stewed legumes
- Stuffed pasta (cheese, meat, or vegetables)
- Veloutés and cream soups

6
FRESH FROM THE SEA
FISH AND SEAFOOD
SAUCES

NANTUA SAUCE

Yield: 6 to 8 servings

3 cups (750 g) béchamel
  sauce, homemade or
  store-bought

1 cup (240 ml) heavy cream

8 ounces (225 g) shrimp,
  peeled, deveined, and
  chopped finely

7 tablespoons (98 g) butter

Salt and fresh-cracked
  black pepper

BEST ON:
- Cooked fish (hot)
- Stuffed pasta
  (seafood or vegetables)

GOES WELL ON:
- Boiled potatoes
- Crespelle
- Crustaceans
- Gnocchi
- Lasagna and cannelloni
- Polenta
- Stewed legumes

1. In a saucepan, combine the béchamel and cream. Cook over low heat, stirring occasionally, until reduced by half.

2. Add the shrimp and cook just until cooked through, about 2 minutes. Remove the pan from heat and immediately add the butter, stirring vigorously to combine and melt the butter.

3. Taste and season with salt and pepper.

DELICATE SHRIMP SAUCE

1. Pour a few swirls of oil into a saucepan and add the chile, parsley, and celery. Cook over medium heat for 3 to 4 minutes until softened and beginning to brown. Add the garlic and cook for about 30 seconds until fragrant.

2. Stir in the cream and tomato purée. Turn the heat to low and simmer for 10 minutes to reduce and thicken the sauce.

3. Add the chopped shrimp to the pan. Cook for about 4 minutes, or until the shrimp are pink and opaque.

4. Taste and season with salt and pepper.

Yield: 6 to 8 servings

Olive oil

1 fresh chile pepper (such as serrano or jalapeño), destemmed, seeded and diced

1 bunch fresh parsley, chopped

1 celery stalk, chopped

1 garlic clove, peeled and minced

1½ cups (360 ml) heavy cream

1½ cups (500 g) tomato purée

2 pounds (908 g) jumbo shrimp or langoustines, peeled, deveined, and coarsely chopped

Salt and fresh-cracked black pepper

BEST ON:
- Cooked pasta (all types)

GOES WELL ON:
- Boiled potatoes
- Cooked fish (hot)
- Crespelle
- Crustaceans
- Gnocchi
- Polenta
- Rice and risotto
- Stewed legumes
- Stuffed pasta (cheese, seafood, or vegetables)

SHRIMP AND ARTICHOKE SAUCE

Yield: 4 servings

Juice of 1 lemon

6 artichokes

Olive oil

2 garlic cloves, peeled
  and minced

1 cup (240 ml) vegetable
  broth

About 10 ounces (280 g)
  shrimp, peeled, deveined,
  and chopped

Salt and fresh-cracked
  black pepper

1 bunch fresh parsley,
  chopped

BEST ON:
- Bruschetta and crostini
- Cooked pasta (any type)
- Crespelle

GOES WELL ON:
- Cooked fish (hot or cold)
- Crustaceans
- Pizza
- Rice and risotto
- Stuffed pasta
  (vegetables or seafood)

1. Fill a large bowl with water and stir in the lemon juice.

2. Cut off the stems from the artichokes, peel them, and cut the stems into thin slices. Soak the stems in the acidulated lemon water until ready to use.

3. Remove the outer leaves from the artichokes and cut off the tips. Halve the artichokes, then quarter them. Remove the barbs and cut the quarters into pieces. Add them to the lemon water.

4. Pour a few swirls of oil into a nonstick skillet and add the garlic. Sauté over medium heat for about 30 seconds until fragrant.

5. Drain the artichokes and add them to the skillet. Pour in the broth, turn the heat to low, and simmer until tender. Transfer half of the artichokes to a food processor or blender, or to a medium-size bowl and use an immersion blender, and blend until smooth. Transfer the remaining artichokes into a bowl.

6. Return the skillet to the stovetop and add the chopped shrimp. Increase the heat to medium-high and cook the shrimp, stirring, for about 2 minutes, or until the shrimp are pink and opaque.

7. Stir in the puréed artichokes and remaining cooked artichokes.

8. Taste and season with salt and pepper, then sprinkle with plenty of parsley.

SHRIMP AND GREEN BEAN SAUCE

Yield: 6 servings

1 pound (454 g) green beans, trimmed

¼ cup (33 g) Soffrito (page 11)

1 pound (454 g) whole shrimp

1 bunch fresh parsley, chopped

Olive oil

Salt and fresh-cracked black pepper

BEST ON:
- Bruschetta and crostini
- Cooked pasta (any type)
- Pasta salad

GOES WELL ON:
- Cooked meats or fish (hot or cold)
- Crustaceans
- Gnocchi
- Pizza, focaccia, piadina
- Raw meats and fish: tartare and carpaccio
- Rice salad
- Veloutés and cream soups

1. Bring a large pot of salted water to a boil, add the green beans, and cook for about 5 minutes until crisp-tender. Drain.

2. Refill the pot with water and bring to a boil. Add the shrimp and blanch for 2 to 3 minutes, depending on the size of your shrimp, until pink. Drain the shrimp, reserving ¼ cup (60 ml) of the cooking water, then peel them, remove the heads, and devein. Finely chop the shrimp.

3. In a food processor or blender, or in a medium-size bowl and using an immersion blender, combine the green beans and soffrito. Blend until thick and creamy, adding a few tablespoons of the reserved cooking water, 1 tablespoon at a time, as needed.

4. Stir in the chopped shrimp and parsley.

5. Taste and season with salt and pepper. If you are serving on bruschetta or crostini, drizzle them with some additional oil before topping them with the sauce.

PRAWN AND ASPARAGUS SAUCE

1. Pour a few swirls of oil into a large skillet and add the garlic clove and asparagus. Sauté over medium heat for 30 seconds to 1 minute until fragrant. Pour in just enough water to cover and bring to a simmer.

2. Remove and discard the garlic and transfer the asparagus mixture to a food processor or blender, or use an immersion blender, and blend until smooth.

3. In the same skillet over medium heat, cook the chopped prawns for about 1 minute, or until they turn pink and are opaque.

4. Stir in the puréed asparagus.

5. Taste and season with salt and pepper.

Yield: 6 servings

Olive oil

1 garlic clove, peeled

1 pound (454 g) asparagus, cut into small pieces

1 pound (454 g) tiger prawns or jumbo shrimp, peeled, deveined, and coarsely chopped

Salt and fresh-cracked black pepper

BEST ON:
- Cooked pasta (all types)
- Crespelle
- Rice and risotto

GOES WELL ON:
- Boiled potatoes
- Bruschetta and crostini
- Cooked fish (hot or cold)
- Crustaceans
- Eggs
- Gnocchi
- Stuffed pasta (cheese, seafood, or vegetables)
- Veloutés and cream soups

RED PRAWN SAUCE

Yield: 4 to 6 servings

1 pound (454 g) king prawns
   or jumbo shrimp

Olive oil

¼ cup (60 ml) dry white wine

2 garlic cloves, peeled

8 ounces (225 g) cherry
   tomatoes, halved

¼ cup (33 g) Soffrito
   (page 11)

1 fresh chile pepper (such
   as serrano or jalapeño),
   destemmed, seeded and
   chopped

1 bunch fresh parsley, chopped

Salt and fresh-cracked
   black pepper

BEST ON:
- Al dente pasta
- Rice and risotto

GOES WELL ON:
- Boiled potatoes
- Bruschetta and crostini
- Gnocchi
- Lasagna and cannelloni
- Pizza, focaccia, piadina

1. Clean, peel, and devein the prawns. Remove their heads, remove the eyes from the heads, and break up the heads. Chop the prawn bodies.

2. Pour a few swirls of oil into a saucepan and add the prawn heads. Cook over medium heat for about 5 minutes, stirring occasionally, or until browned.

3. Pour in the wine to deglaze the pan, scraping up any browned bits from the bottom. Cook for 20 minutes, stirring occasionally. Crush the heads with a wooden spoon, then strain the mixture through a fine-mesh sieve set over a heat proof bowl, reserving the liquid. Discard the solids.

4. Return the saucepan to medium heat, pour in a few swirls of oil, and add the garlic cloves. Sauté for 2 to 3 minutes until beginning to brown.

5. Stir in the tomatoes, soffrito, strained prawn head cooking liquid, chile, and a handful of parsley. Turn the heat to high and cook, stirring frequently, for 10 minutes.

6. Stir in the chopped prawns and cook for 2 minutes, stirring occasionally, or until cooked through and opaque. Remove and discard the garlic.

7. Taste and season with salt and pepper, then sprinkle with the remaining parsley.

PRAWN AND PEA SAUCE

1. Clean, peel, and devein the prawns. Remove their heads, remove the eyes from the heads, and break up the heads. Chop the prawn bodies.

2. Pour a few swirls of oil into a saucepan and add the prawn heads. Cook over medium heat for about 5 minutes, stirring occasionally, or until browned.

3. Pour in the wine to deglaze the pan, scraping up any browned bits from the bottom. Cook for 20 minutes, stirring occasionally. Crush the heads with a wooden spoon, then strain the mixture through a fine-mesh sieve set over a heat proof bowl, reserving the liquid. Discard the solids.

4. Return the saucepan to medium heat, pour in a few swirls of oil, and add the garlic cloves and chile. Sauté for 2 to 3 minutes until the chile softens and the garlic begins to brown.

5. Stir in the strained prawn head cooking liquid, soffrito, peas, and parsley. Turn the heat to high and cook for 2 minutes, stirring frequently.

6. Stir in the chopped prawns and cook for 2 minutes, stirring occasionally, or until cooked through and opaque. Remove and discard the garlic.

7. Taste and season with salt and pepper.

Yield: 4 servings

1 pound (454 g) king prawns or jumbo shrimp

Olive oil

¼ cup (60 ml) dry white wine

2 garlic cloves, peeled

1 fresh chile pepper (such as serrano or jalapeño), destemmed, seeded and finely chopped

¼ cup (33 g) Soffrito (page 11)

8 ounces (225 g) shelled peas, fresh or frozen and thawed

1 bunch fresh parsley, chopped

Salt and fresh-cracked black pepper

BEST ON:
- Cooked pasta (all types)
- Gnocchi
- Rice and risotto

GOES WELL ON:
- Boiled potatoes
- Bruschetta and crostini
- Crespelle
- Polenta

SQUID AND CHERRY TOMATO SAUCE

Yield: 4 servings

Olive oil

2 large garlic cloves, crushed

1 fresh chile pepper (such as serrano or jalapeño), destemmed, seeded and diced, or 1 teaspoon red pepper flakes

1½ pounds (681 g) squid, thawed if frozen, cleaned and cut into small pieces

12 ounces (340 g) cherry tomatoes, chopped

½ cup (120 ml) white wine

¼ cup (33 g) Soffrito (page 11)

Salt and fresh-cracked black pepper

1 bunch fresh parsley, chopped

1. Pour a few swirls of oil into a large skillet and add the garlic cloves and chile. Sauté over medium heat for 1 to 2 minutes, or until golden and fragrant.

2. Add the squid, cherry tomatoes, wine, and soffrito. Turn the heat to low and cook for about 30 minutes or until the squid is opaque and tender. Remove and discard the garlic.

3. Taste and season with salt and pepper, then sprinkle with plenty of parsley.

BEST ON:
- Cooked pasta (all types)
- Polenta

GOES WELL ON:
- Boiled potatoes
- Cooked fish (hot)
- Crespelle
- Crustaceans
- Gnocchi
- Rice and risotto
- Stuffed pasta (cheese, seafood, or vegetables)
- Veloutés and cream soups

SQUID SAUCE

Yield: 4 servings

Olive oil

2 large garlic cloves, crushed

1 fresh chile pepper (such
 as serrano or jalapeño),
 stemmed and diced, or
 1 teaspoon red pepper flakes

1 tablespoon (15 g)
 tomato paste

½ cup (120 ml) water

1½ pounds (681 g) squid,
 thawed if frozen, cleaned
 and cut into small pieces

½ cup (120 ml) white wine

¼ cup (33 g) Soffrito
 (page 11)

Salt and fresh-cracked
 black pepper

1 bunch fresh parsley, chopped

1. Pour a few swirls of oil into a large skillet and add the garlic cloves and chile. Sauté over medium heat for 1 to 2 minutes, or until golden and fragrant.

2. In a small bowl, stir together the tomato paste and water until the tomato paste dissolves.

3. Add the squid, wine, tomato paste mixture, and soffrito to the skillet. Turn the heat to low and cook for about 20 to 25 minutes, or until the squid is opaque and tender. Remove and discard the garlic.

4. Taste and season with salt and pepper, then sprinkle with plenty of parsley.

BEST ON:
- Cooked pasta (all types)
- Rice and risotto

GOES WELL ON:
- Cook seafood (hot)
- Crespelle
- Eggs
- Gnocchi
- Polenta
- Stuffed pasta (cheese, seafood, or vegetables)
- Veloutés and cream soups

SQUID, OLIVE, AND CAPER SAUCE

1. Pour a few swirls of oil into a large skillet and add the garlic cloves and chile. Sauté over medium heat for 1 to 2 minutes, or until golden and fragrant.

2. Add the squid, wine, chopped olives, capers, and soffrito. Turn the heat to low and cook for about 30 minutes, or until the squid is opaque and tender. Remove and discard the garlic.

3. Taste and season with salt and pepper, then sprinkle with oregano leaves.

Yield: 4 servings

Olive oil

2 large garlic cloves, crushed

1 fresh chile pepper (such as serrano or jalapeño), destemmed, seeded and diced, or 1 teaspoon red pepper flakes

1½ pounds (681 g) squid, thawed if frozen, cleaned and cut into small pieces

½ cup (120 ml) white wine

½ cup (50 g) pitted black olives, chopped

3 tablespoons (27 g) salt-packed capers, rinsed

¼ cup (33 g) Soffrito (page 11)

Salt and fresh-cracked black pepper

1 bunch fresh oregano

BEST ON:
- Cooked pasta (all types)
- Gnocchi

GOES WELL ON:
- Crespelle
- Crustaceans
- Lasagna and cannelloni
- Polenta
- Rice and risotto
- Stewed legumes

CLAM SAUCE

Yield: 4 servings

2 pounds (908 g) clams

Salt

Olive oil

2 garlic cloves, peeled and
finely chopped

1 fresh chile pepper (such
as serrano or jalapeño),
destemmed, seeded
and diced

1 bunch fresh parsley, minced

¼ cup (60 ml) dry white wine

2 tablespoons (16 g)
Soffrito (page 11)

Fresh-cracked black pepper

BEST ON:
- Al dente pasta

GOES WELL ON:
- Cooked fish (hot)
- Crustaceans
- Pizza, focaccia, piadina
- Rice and risotto
- Stuffed pasta (cheese,
  seafood, or vegetables)

1. Scrub the clams. In a large bowl, combine the clams and enough water to cover by a few inches. Generously salt the water and stir to combine. Let sit overnight in the refrigerator to release their sand and debris.

2. Carefully scoop the clams from the water, leaving the dirt and sand behind. Rinse and drain the clams, discarding any that are cracked or broken, or that will not close when tapped.

3. Pour a few swirls of oil into a skillet and add the garlic, chile, and half of the parsley. Sauté for about 1 minute until fragrant and the garlic and chile begin to soften.

4. Add the clams and pour in the wine. Cover and cook until the clams open (cook time will vary based on the type and size of clams used). Discard any clams that do not open.

5. Remove the clams. Strain the cooking liquid through a fine-mesh sieve set over a bowl and discard the solids.

6. Shell the clams and add the meat to the strained liquid. Stir in the soffrito and sprinkle with the remaining parsley.

7. Taste and season generously with pepper.

RED CLAM SAUCE

1. Scrub the clams. In a large bowl, combine the clams and enough water to cover by a few inches. Generously salt the water and stir to combine. Let sit overnight in the refrigerator to release their sand and debris.

2. Carefully scoop the clams from the water, leaving the dirt and sand behind. Rinse and drain the clams, discarding any that are cracked or broken, or that will not close when tapped.

3. Pour a few swirls of oil into a skillet and add the garlic, chile, and parsley. Sauté over medium heat for about 1 minute until fragrant and the garlic and chile begin to soften.

4. Stir in the tomato purée and simmer for 20 minutes to reduce the sauce.

5. Add the clams, cover the skillet, and cook until the clams open (cook time will vary based on the type and size of the clams used). Discard any clams that do not open.

6. Shell the clams and return the meat to the sauce. Stir in the soffrito.

7. Taste and season generously with pepper.

Yield: 4 servings

2 pounds (908 g) clams

Salt

Olive oil

2 garlic cloves, peeled and finely chopped

1 fresh chile pepper (such as serrano or jalapeño), destemmed, seeded and finely chopped

1 bunch fresh parsley, chopped

2½ cups (625 g) tomato purée

2 tablespoons (16 g) Soffrito (page 11)

Fresh-cracked black pepper

BEST ON:
- Al dente spaghetti
- Pizza, focaccia, piadina

GOES WELL ON:
- Crespelle
- Crustaceans
- Gnocchi
- Rice and risotto
- Stewed legumes
- Stuffed pasta (seafood or vegetables)

CLAM AND SALMON ROE SAUCE

Yield: 4 servings

2 pounds (908 g) clams

Salt

Olive oil

2 garlic cloves, peeled and finely chopped

1 fresh chile pepper (such as serrano or jalapeño), destemmed, seeded and finely chopped

1 bunch fresh parsley, chopped

1 cup (240 ml) heavy cream

2 tablespoons (11 g) sautéed onion

Fresh-cracked black pepper

½ cup (128 g) salmon roe

BEST ON:
- Al dente spaghetti

GOES WELL ON:
- Crespelle
- Crustaceans
- Gnocchi
- Rice and risotto
- Stewed legumes
- Stuffed pasta (seafood or vegetables)

1. Scrub the clams. In a large bowl, combine the clams and enough water to cover by a few inches. Generously salt the water and stir to combine. Let sit overnight in the refrigerator to release their sand and debris.

2. Carefully scoop the clams from the water, leaving the dirt and sand behind. Rinse and drain the clams, discarding any that are cracked or broken, or that will not close when tapped.

3. Pour a few swirls of oil into a skillet and add the garlic, chile, and parsley. Sauté over medium heat for about 1 minute until fragrant and the garlic and chile begin to soften.

4. Add the clams, cover the skillet, and cook until the clams open (cook time will vary based on the type and size of the clams used). Discard any clams that do not open.

5. Remove the clams. Strain the cooking liquid through a fine-mesh sieve set over a bowl and discard the solids.

6. Shell the clams and add the meat to the strained liquid, along with the cream and sautéed onion. Stir to combine.

7. Taste and season generously with pepper. Scatter the salmon roe over the sauce.

CLAM AND VEGETABLE SAUCE

1. Scrub the clams. In a large bowl, combine the clams and enough water to cover by a few inches. Generously salt the water and stir to combine. Let sit overnight in the refrigerator to release their sand and debris.

2. Carefully scoop the clams from the water, leaving the dirt and sand behind. Rinse and drain the clams, discarding any that are cracked or broken, or that will not close when tapped.

3. Pour a few swirls of oil into a skillet and add the garlic, chile, and parsley. Sauté over medium heat for about 1 minute until fragrant and the garlic and chile begin to soften.

4. Add the clams, cover the skillet, and cook until the clams open (cook time will vary based on the type and size of the clams used). Discard any clams that do not open.

5. Remove the clams. Strain the cooking liquid through a fine-mesh sieve set over a bowl and discard the solids.

6. Shell the clams and add the meat to the strained liquid, along with the puréed vegetables. Stir to combine.

7. Taste and season generously with pepper.

Yield: 4 servings

2 pounds (908 g) clams

Salt

Olive oil

2 garlic cloves, peeled and finely chopped

1 fresh chile pepper (such as serrano or jalapeño), destemmed, seeded and finely chopped

1 bunch fresh parsley, chopped

1 cup (240 ml) puréed cooked vegetables (any vegetables you like, 10% of which should be onion)

Fresh-cracked black pepper

BEST ON:
- Cooked pasta (all types)
- Gnocchi

GOES WELL ON:
- Boiled potatoes
- Crustaceans
- Rice and risotto
- Stuffed pasta (cheese, seafood, or vegetables)
- Veloutés and cream soups

CIOPPINO

Yield: 4 servings

4 salt-packed anchovies, or
    2 teaspoons anchovy paste

1 pound (454 g) mixed white
    fish fillets (such as bass, cod,
    haddock, snapper, tilapia)

Olive oil

1 white onion, diced

1 celery stalk, diced

1 carrot, diced

1 bunch fresh parsley,
    chopped

½ cup (120 ml) white wine

½ cup (125 g) tomato purée

Salt and fresh-cracked
    black pepper

BEST ON:
- Cooked pasta (all types)

GOES WELL ON:
- Cooked fish (hot)
- Crespelle
- Crustaceans
- Gnocchi
- Polenta
- Stuffed pasta (cheese,
  seafood, or vegetables)

1. Remove any bones, heads, and tails from the anchovies and rinse them under running water.

2. Clean, skin, and debone the white fish, as needed, and chop it coarsely.

3. Pour a few swirls of oil into a large saucepan and add the anchovies, onion, celery, carrot, and half of the parsley. Sauté over medium heat for about 5 minutes until the vegetables soften and begin to brown.

4. Pour in the wine to deglaze the pan, scraping up any browned bits from the bottom. Simmer for about 3 minutes until the wine evaporates.

5. Stir in the tomato purée and add the white fish. Turn the heat to low and cook for 5 minutes, or until the fish is cooked through and flakes easily with a fork. Transfer half of the sauce to a food processor or blender, or a medium-size bowl and use an immersion blender, and blend until smooth. Return the sauce to the pan.

6. Taste and season with salt and pepper. Let simmer for about 5 minutes to reduce and thicken. Sprinkle with the remaining parsley.

CAVIAR SAUCE

Yield: 4 servings

⅓ cup (80 ml) leftover roast beef juices or beef stock

½ cup (120 l) heavy cream

3 tablespoons (48 g) caviar (sturgeon roe is perfect but expensive, or another roe)

BEST ON:
- Bruschetta and crostini
- Cooked pasta (all types, especially egg pasta)

GOES WELL ON:
- Boiled potatoes
- Cooked fish (hot)
- Cooked vegetables

1. In a small saucepan, combine the roast beef juices and cream. Cook over medium heat, whisking, until emulsified.

2. Add the caviar and stir well—the sauce will turn a pale green color.

SEAFOOD SAUCE

Yield: 8 to 10 servings

1. Scrub the clams and mussels and scrape away the mussels' beards with a knife. In a very large bowl, combine the clams and mussels with enough water to cover by a few inches. Generously salt the water and stir to combine. Let sit overnight in the refrigerator to release their sand and debris.

2. Carefully scoop the clams and mussels from the water, leaving the dirt and sand behind. Rinse and drain the clams and mussels, discarding any that are cracked or broken, or that will not close when tapped.

3. Pour a few swirls of oil a large saucepan and add the garlic, chile, and half of the parsley. Sauté over medium heat for about 2 minutes until the mixture softens and begin to brown.

4. Add the mussels and clams and cook until they open (cook time will vary based on the size of your shellfish). Discard any that do not open. Remove the mussels and clams, shell them, and chop the meat into pieces.

5. Strain the cooking liquid through a fine-mesh sieve set over a heatproof bowl. Clean the pan and return it to medium heat and pour in a few swirls of oil.

6. Chop the cuttlefish and scallops and add them to the pan. Sauté for 2 minutes.

7. Pour in the wine to deglaze the pan, scraping up any browned bits from the bottom. Simmer for about 3 minutes until the wine evaporates.

8. Stir in the soffrito, mussels, clams, and, if you wish, a little of the strained cooking liquid (do not throw it away; it makes an excellent broth).

9. Taste and season with salt and pepper, then sprinkle with the remaining parsley.

2 pounds (908 g) clams

2 pounds (908 g) mussels

Salt and fresh-cracked black pepper

Olive oil

2 garlic cloves, peeled and finely chopped

1 fresh chile pepper (such as serrano or jalapeño), destemmed, seeded and finely chopped

1 bunch fresh parsley, chopped

8 cuttlefish or firm white fish fillets

8 scallops

¼ cup (60 ml) white wine

¼ cup (33 g) Soffrito (page 11)

BEST ON:
- Al dente spaghetti

GOES WELL ON:
- Cooked pasta (all types)
- Gnocchi
- Rice and risotto
- Stewed legumes
- Stuffed pasta (cheese, seafood, or vegetables

SEAFOOD AND LOBSTER SAUCE

Yield: 4 to 6 servings

2 pounds (908 g) clams

2 pounds (908 g) mussels

Salt and fresh-cracked
   black pepper

Olive oil

1 fresh chile pepper (such
   as serrano or jalapeño),
   destemmed, seeded and
   finely chopped

1 bunch fresh parsley, finely
   chopped

2 garlic cloves, peeled and
   finely chopped

Meat from 1 whole
   cooked lobster

¼ cup (60 ml) white wine

¼ cup (33 g) Soffrito
   (page 11)

BEST ON:
- Al dente spaghetti

GOES WELL ON:
- Bruschetta and crostini
- Crespelle
- Gnocchi
- Polenta
- Veloutés and cream soups

1. Scrub the clams and mussels and scrape away the mussels' beards with a knife. In a large bowl, combine the clams and mussels with enough water to cover by a few inches. Generously salt the water and stir to combine. Let sit overnight in the refrigerator to release their sand and debris.

2. Carefully scoop the clams and mussels from the water, leaving the dirt and sand behind. Rinse and drain the clams and mussels, discarding any that are cracked or broken, or that will not close when tapped.

3. Pour a few swirls of oil into a large pot and add the chile and half of the parsley. Cook over medium heat for 1 to 2 minutes, stirring occasionally, until beginning to soften and brown. Add the garlic and sauté for about 30 seconds until fragrant.

4. Add the clams and mussels and cook until they open (cook time will vary based on the size of the shellfish you use). Discard any clams or mussels that do not open.

5. Remove the mussels and clams, shell them, and chop the meat into pieces.

6. Strain the cooking liquid through a fine-mesh sieve set over a heatproof bowl (do not throw it away; it makes an excellent broth).

7. Combine the lobster meat in a skillet with a few swirls of oil over medium-high heat. Cook for 2 minutes, stirring, or until browned.

8. Pour in the wine to deglaze the skillet, scraping up any browned bits from the bottom. Simmer for about 3 minutes until the wine evaporates.

9. Stir in the soffrito, clams, mussels, and a little of the strained cooking liquid.

10. Taste and season with salt and pepper, then sprinkle with the remaining parsley.

SEAFOOD CARBONARA

Yield: 4 to 6 servings

About 10 ounces (280 g) fish
   fillets of choice, diced

Olive oil

5 large egg yolks

½ cup (50 g) grated
   grana (such as Asiago,
   Parmigiano-Reggiano,
   or Pecorino Romano)

Fresh-cracked black pepper

BEST ON:
- Al dente pasta

GOES WELL ON:
- Gnocchi

1. Place the fish in a skillet with a few swirls of oil. Sauté over high heat for 2 to 3 minutes until cooked through and opaque.

2. In a large bowl, whisk the egg yolks while adding the cheese a bit at a time until blended and combined.

3. Generously season with pepper and whisk to combine.

4. When dressing the hot pasta with the sauce, which will cook the eggs gently from its residual heat, add about ½ cup (120 ml) of the pasta cooking water, as needed, for a creamier texture, and the sautéed fish and stir gently to coat and combine. If you're concerned about uncooked egg, combine everything in the skillet and cook gently over low heat for about 1 minute, stirring constantly, to cook the egg.

RED SEA BASS SAUCE

1. Remove the skin and any bones from the fillets and cut the fish into small pieces.

2. Prepare an ice bath. Score the tomatoes with an X on the bottom to make them easier to peel. Bring a large pot of water to a boil, add the tomatoes, and cook for about 1 minute, or until the skins start to peel back in the place where you scored them. Using a slotted spoon, transfer the tomatoes to the ice bath. When cool enough to handle, peel the tomatoes, halve them, remove the seeds, and coarsely chop them.

3. Pour a few swirls of oil into a saucepan, add the garlic, and cook over medium heat for 30 seconds to 1 minute, or until golden brown and fragrant.

4. Stir in the tomatoes, turn the heat to high, and cook for 5 minutes.

5. Turn the heat to medium, add the fish and soffrito, and simmer for about 6 to 8 minutes, or until the fish is just cooked through and flakes easily with a fork.

6. Taste and season with salt and pepper, then stir in the parsley.

1 pound (454 g) red sea bass, red snapper, or grouper fillets

2 large fresh tomatoes

Olive oil

1 garlic clove, peeled and finely chopped

2 tablespoons (16 g) Soffrito (page 11)

Salt and fresh-cracked black pepper

1 bunch fresh parsley, finely chopped

BEST ON:
- Cooked fish (hot)
- Cooked pasta (all types)
- Stuffed pasta (cheese, seafood, or vegetables)

GOES WELL ON:
- Boiled potatoes
- Bruschetta and crostini
- Crespelle
- Crustaceans
- Gnocchi
- Lasagna and cannelloni
- Rice and risotto
- Stewed legumes

TUNA AND EGGPLANT SAUCE

Yield: 4 to 6 servings

1 garlic clove, peeled
    and finely chopped

Olive oil

8 ounces (225 g) peeled
    whole tomatoes, fresh
    or canned

2 tablespoons (16 g)
    Soffrito (page 11)

1 bunch fresh basil, chopped

Salt and fresh-cracked
    black pepper

Sunflower seed oil

1 pound (454 g) eggplant,
    cubed

1 cup (205 g) oil-packed tuna

1. Add the garlic to a saucepan with a few swirls of olive oil. Sauté over medium heat for about 30 seconds until fragrant.

2. Add the tomatoes, soffrito, and basil to the pan. Season with salt and pepper to taste. Cook for 10 minutes, stirring occasionally to help break up the tomatoes.

3. In a large skillet, heat a few tablespoons (45 ml) of sunflower seed oil over medium-high heat until shimmering. Add the eggplant and sauté for 2 to 3 minutes until golden brown. Using a slotted spoon, transfer to paper towel to drain, then toss the eggplant in the saucepan with the tomatoes.

4. Drain the tuna well and stir it into the sauce. Cook for 2 minutes to heat through.

5. Taste and season with salt and pepper.

BEST ON:
- Cooked pasta (all types)

GOES WELL ON:
- Cooked fish (hot)
- Crespelle
- Crustaceans
- Gnocchi
- Pizza, focaccia, piadina
- Polenta
- Rice and risotto
- Stewed legumes
- Stuffed pasta (cheese, seafood, or vegetables)
- Veloutés and cream soups

TUNA SAUCE LUANA STYLE

1. Drain the tuna and pour it into a bowl.

2. Season with a drizzle of oil and salt and pepper to taste.

3. Zest the lemons (save the lemons for another use) into the bowl and stir to combine.

4. If desired, you can enhance this sauce with pickles or marinated artichoke hearts to taste, well drained and chopped.

Yield: 4 to 6 servings

1⅓ cups (273 g) oil-packed tuna

Olive oil

Salt and fresh-cracked
 black pepper

4 organic lemons

BEST ON:
- Al dente pasta
- Bruschetta and crostini

GOES WELL ON:
- Boiled potatoes
- Pasta salad
- Rice and risotto
- Rice salad

TUNA AND MOZZARELLA SAUCE

Yield: 4 to 6 servings

1⅓ cups (273 g) oil-packed tuna

1⅓ cups (153 g) finely chopped mozzarella cheese

1 bunch fresh basil, chopped

Olive oil

Salt and ground white pepper

BEST ON:
- Al dente pasta
- Bruschetta and crostini
- Pasta salad

GOES WELL ON:
- Boiled potatoes
- Pizza, focaccia, piadina
- Rice and risotto
- Rice salad

1. Drain the tuna and place it in a medium-size bowl.

2. Gently stir in the mozzarella.

3. Stir the basil into the sauce. Pour in a few swirls of oil and mix to coat and combine.

4. Taste and season with salt and white pepper.

5. If you like, you can enhance this sauce with diced cherry tomatoes, fresh chile peppers, and pitted black olives.

FRESH TUNA AND PISTACHIO SAUCE

Yield: 4 to 6 servings

1. Mince together the fresh tuna and garlic. Place the mixture in a skillet, pour in a few swirls of oil, and sauté over medium-high heat for 1 minute to sear.

2. Stir in the pistachios.

3. Taste and season with salt and pepper.

4. If you like, you can also add diced onion, carrots, and celery, sautéed first in a little oil.

1 pound (454 g) fresh tuna fillet

2 garlic cloves, peeled

Olive oil

1½ cups (184 g) shelled roasted and salted pistachios, chopped

Salt and fresh-cracked black pepper

BEST ON:
- Al dente pasta

GOES WELL ON:
- Boiled potatoes
- Bruschetta and crostini
- Crustaceans
- Pizza, focaccia, piadina
- Polenta
- Rice and risotto
- Stuffed pasta (cheese, seafood, or vegetables)
- Veloutés and cream soups

FRESH TUNA SAUCE WITH ToMATOES

Yield: 4 servings

2 large fresh tomatoes

Olive oil

1 garlic clove, peeled and finely chopped

1 pound (454 g) fresh tuna fillet, diced

Salt and fresh-cracked black pepper

1 bunch fresh parsley, chopped

BEST ON:
- Al dente pasta

GOES WELL ON:
- Boiled potatoes
- Bruschetta and crostini
- Crespelle
- Gnocchi
- Lasagna and cannelloni
- Pizza, focaccia, piadina
- Polenta
- Rice and risotto
- Stuffed pasta (cheese, seafood, or vegetables)
- Veloutés and cream soups

1. Prepare an ice bath. Score the tomatoes with an X on the bottom to make them easier to peel. Bring a large pot of water to a boil, add the tomatoes, and cook for about 1 minute, or until the skins start to peel back in the place where you scored them. Using a slotted spoon, transfer the tomatoes to the ice bath. When cool enough to handle, peel the tomatoes, halve them, remove the seeds, and coarsely chop them.

2. Pour a few swirls of oil into a saucepan and add the garlic. Sauté over medium heat for about 30 seconds until golden and fragrant.

3. Add the tomatoes, turn the heat to high, and cook for 15 minutes, stirring occasionally.

4. Stir the tuna into the sauce and cook for 2 minutes.

5. Taste and season with salt and pepper, then stir in the parsley.

TUNA AND BEAN SAUCE

1. In a food processor or blender, or in a medium-size bowl and using an immersion blender, blend half of the beans until creamy.

2. Put the remaining whole beans in a medium-size bowl and season them with a few swirls of oil, or to taste.

3. Stir the tuna into the whole beans, along with the lemon zest.

4. Stir in the bean purée.

5. Taste and season with salt and pepper.

Yield: 4 to 6 servings

1½ cups (273 g) cooked cannellini beans or canned, rinsed, and drained

Olive oil

1½ cups (308 g) canned drained tuna, chopped

Grated zest of 1 organic lemon

Salt and fresh-cracked black pepper

BEST ON:
- Bruschetta or crostini
- Pasta salad

GOES WELL ON:
- Cooked fish (hot or cold)
- Cooked pasta (any type)
- Rice salad
- Veloutés and cream soups

SMOKED SALMON AND RICOTTA SAUCE

Yield: 4 to 6 servings

1 bunch fresh chives,
   finely chopped

8 ounces (225 g) smoked
   salmon, finely chopped

1 pound (454 g) ricotta
   (preferably sheep's milk)

1 tablespoon (15 g)
   Tomato Sauce (page 98),
   or store-bought

Olive oil

Salt and fresh-cracked
   black pepper

BEST ON:
- Cooked pasta (all types)

GOES WELL ON:
- Bruschetta and crostini
- Lasagna and cannelloni
- Pizza, focaccia, piadina
- Stuffed pasta (cheese,
  seafood, or vegetables)
- Veloutés and cream soups

1. Add the chives and salmon to a large bowl.

2. Add the ricotta and tomato sauce.

3. Generously drizzle with oil and season with salt and pepper.

4. Whisk vigorously to combine.

SARDINE, PINE NUT, AND RAISIN SAUCE

Yield: 4 servings

½ cup (70 g) pine nuts

½ cup (73 g) raisins

1 very large bunch wild fennel fronds or fronds and stalks from 2 large fennel bulbs

1 white onion, chopped

Olive oil

1 pound (454 g) fresh sardine fillets, diced

2 tablespoons (16 g) Soffrito (page 11)

Salt and fresh-cracked black pepper

BEST ON:
- Cooked pasta (all types)

GOES WELL ON:
- Bruschetta and crostini
- Cooked fish (hot)
- Crustaceans
- Gnocchi
- Pizza, focaccia, piadina
- Polenta
- Stuffed pasta (cheese, seafood, or vegetables)

1. In a small nonstick skillet over medium-high heat, toast the pine nuts for 2 to 3 minutes until lightly browned and fragrant. Set aside.

2. In a medium-size bowl, combine the raisins with enough hot water to cover and let soak until needed. Drain and squeeze the excess liquid from the raisins.

3. Bring a saucepan full of water to a boil. Add the wild fennel and blanch for 2 minutes. Drain, reserving ¼ cup (60 ml) of the cooking water, and transfer to a food processor or blender. Blend until smooth, adding a bit of cooking water at a time if needed.

4. Add the onion to a skillet and pour in a few swirls of oil. Sauté over high heat for 2 minutes until the onion begins to soften and brown. Add the sardines and sauté for 2 minutes.

5. Stir in the wild fennel purée, soffrito, soaked raisins, and the pine nuts. Turn the heat to medium and cook for about 5 minutes to heat through.

6. Taste and season with salt and pepper.

SARDINE ToMATO SAUCE

1. Bring a saucepan full of water to a boil. Add the wild fennel and blanch for 2 minutes. Drain, reserving ¼ cup (60 ml) of the cooking water, and transfer to a food processor or blender. Blend until smooth, adding a bit of cooking water at a time if needed.

2. Add the onion to a skillet and pour in a few swirls of oil. Sauté over high heat for 2 minutes until the onion begins to soften and brown.

3. Using a wooden spoon, stir in the anchovies, turn the heat to medium, and cook for about 3 minutes, stirring, until the anchovies melt.

4. In a small bowl, stir together the tomato paste and water until the tomato paste dissolves. Add this to the skillet, along with the soffrito and sardines. Cook until the sardines are soft, stirring occasionally.

5. Stir in the wild fennel purée and cook for 2 minutes to heat through.

6. Taste and season with salt and pepper.

Yield: 4 servings

1 bunch wild fennel or stalks and fronds from 1 large fennel bulb

1 white onion, chopped

Olive oil

4 oil-packed anchovy fillets, or 2 teaspoons anchovy paste

1 cup (240 g) tomato paste

1 cup (240 ml) water

2 tablespoons (16 g) Soffrito (page 11)

1 pound (454 g) fresh sardine fillets, finely chopped

Salt and fresh-cracked black pepper

BEST ON:
- Cooked pasta (all types)

GOES WELL ON:
- Boiled potatoes
- Bruschetta and crostini
- Crustaceans
- Gnocchi
- Pizza, focaccia, piadina
- Polenta
- Stuffed pasta (cheese, seafood, or vegetables)

MONKFISH SAUCE

Yield: 4 to 6 servings

1 pound (455 g) monkfish
   tails

Olive oil

1 garlic clove, peeled
   and minced

About 10 ounces (280 g)
   cherry tomatoes, coarsely
   chopped

1 bunch fresh basil, chopped

2 tablespoons (16 g) Soffrito
   (page 11)

Salt and fresh-cracked
   black pepper

BEST ON:
- Cooked pasta (all types)
- Stuffed pasta (cheese,
  seafood, or vegetables)

GOES WELL ON:
- Boiled potatoes
- Cooked fish (hot)
- Crespelle
- Crustaceans
- Gnocchi
- Lasagna and cannelloni
- Polenta
- Rice and risotto
- Stewed legumes

1. Remove the skin and any bones from the monkfish tails and cut them into chunks.

2. Pour a few swirls of oil into a saucepan and add the garlic. Sauté over medium heat for about 30 seconds until fragrant and beginning to brown.

3. Add the tomatoes, turn the heat to high, and cook for 5 minutes.

4. Add the basil to the pan along with the monkfish. Stir in the soffrito and cook for 3 minutes, stirring until the fish is cooked through and the tomatoes are softened.

5. Taste and season with salt and pepper.

SWORDFISH SAUCE

1. Add the onion and parsley to a skillet. Pour in a few swirls of oil and sauté over medium heat for 2 to 3 minutes until the onion softens.

2. Stir in the tomato purée and soffrito.

3. Add the swordfish, turn the heat to low, and cook for 20 minutes, stirring occasionally, until the swordfish is cooked through and opaque and the sauce is thickened.

4. Taste and season with salt and pepper.

Yield: 6 to 8 servings

1 white onion, chopped

1 bunch fresh parsley, chopped

Olive oil

2½ cups (625 g) tomato purée

2 tablespoons (16 g) Soffrito (page 11)

1½ pounds (681 g) swordfish belly, cubed

Salt and fresh-cracked black pepper

BEST ON:
- Cooked pasta (all types)
- Gnocchi

GOES WELL ON:
- Boiled potatoes
- Cooked fish (hot)
- Crespelle
- Polenta
- Rice and risotto
- Stuffed pasta (cheese, seafood, or vegetables)

SWORDFISH AND WILD FENNEL MEATBALLS IN TOMATO SAUCE

Yield: 4 servings

12 ounces (340 g) swordfish fillet, skin and bones removed as needed, roughly chopped

1 bunch wild fennel fronds, or fronds from 1 or 2 fennel bulbs, roughly chopped

2 egg whites

Chili powder for seasoning

Salt and fresh-cracked black pepper

1½ cups (175 g) bread crumbs, plus more as needed

Sunflower seed oil

1 cup (245 g) Tomato Sauce (page 98), or store-bought

BEST ON:
- Cooked pasta (all types)
- Stuffed pasta (cheese, vegetables, or seafood)

GOES WELL ON:
- Boiled potatoes
- Gnocchi
- Pizza, focaccia, piadina
- Polenta
- Stewed legumes

1. In a food processor or blender, or in a medium-size bowl and using an immersion blender, combine the swordfish, fennel fronds, 1 egg white, and a pinch of chili powder. Blend until smooth. Season with salt and pepper and pulse to combine.

2. In a shallow bowl, whisk the remaining egg white. Pour the bread crumbs into another shallow bowl.

3. With slightly wet hands, form small (about 1-inch, or 2.5 cm) balls from the swordfish mixture and dip them first in the egg white and then in the bread crumbs to coat. Place the coated balls on a plate. Line a sheet pan with paper towels.

4. In a large skillet, heat about 2 inches (5 cm) of sunflower seed oil over medium-high heat until shimmering. Carefully add the swordfish balls to the hot oil, working in batches if needed so the pan is not crowded, and fry until browned, turning occasionally. Transfer the cooked swordfish balls to the prepared sheet pan to drain.

5. Pour the tomato sauce into a saucepan, add the swordfish balls, and cook over medium heat for 5 minutes to warm the sauce.

6. Taste and season with salt and pepper.

COD AND ARTICHOKE SAUCE

1. Fill a large bowl with water and stir in the lemon juice.

2. Cut off the stems from the artichokes, peel them, and cut the stems into thin slices. Soak the stems in the acidulated lemon water until ready to use.

3. Remove the outer leaves from the artichokes and cut off the tips. Halve the artichokes, then quarter them. Remove the barbs and cut the quarters into pieces. Add them to the lemon water.

4. Pour a few swirls of oil into a nonstick skillet and add the garlic. Sauté over medium heat for about 30 seconds until fragrant.

5. Drain the artichokes and add them to the skillet. Pour in the broth, turn the heat to low, and simmer until tender. Transfer half of the artichokes to a food processor or blender, or to a medium-size bowl and use an immersion blender, and blend until smooth. Transfer the remaining artichokes into a bowl.

6. Return the skillet to medium heat and add the cod. Cook for about 2 minutes per side, or until the cod is opaque and flakes easily with a fork.

7. Stir in the puréed artichokes and remaining cooked artichokes.

8. Taste and season with salt and pepper, then sprinkle with plenty of chopped parsley.

Yield: 4 servings

Juice of 1 lemon

6 artichokes

Olive oil

2 garlic cloves, peeled and minced

1 cup (240 ml) vegetable broth

About 10 ounces (280 g) cod fillets, cut into chunks

Salt and fresh-cracked black pepper

1 bunch fresh parsley, chopped

BEST ON:
- Cooked pasta (all types)
- Gnocchi

GOES WELL ON:
- Cook seafood (hot)
- Lasagna and cannelloni
- Polenta
- Rice and risotto
- Stewed legumes
- Stuffed pasta (cheese, seafood, or vegetables)

7

HEARTY MEAT SAUCES

AMATRICIANA SAUCE

Yield: 4 servings

1 pound (454 g) fresh San Marzano or Roma tomatoes, or 1 (14.5-ounce, or 410 g) can whole peeled San Marzano tomatoes

1 tablespoon (14 g) lard or butter

1 fresh red chile pepper (such as Fresno), destemmed, seeded and chopped, or 1 teaspoon red pepper flakes

8 ounces (225 g) guanciale, pancetta, or bacon, cut into strips

¾ cup (75 g) grated Pecorino Romano cheese

Salt and black pepper

BEST ON:
- Cooked pasta (all types)

GOES WELL ON:
- Gnocchi
- Lasagna and cannelloni
- Polenta
- Rice and risotto
- Stewed legumes
- Stuffed pasta (cheese, meat, or vegetables)

1. If using fresh tomatoes, prepare an ice bath. Score the tomatoes with an X on the bottom to make them easier to peel. Bring a large pot of water to a boil, add the tomatoes, and cook for about 1 minute, or until the skins start to peel back in the place where you scored them. Using a slotted spoon, transfer the tomatoes to the ice bath. When cool enough to handle, peel the tomatoes, halve them, remove the seeds, and chop them.

2. In a skillet over high heat, melt the lard. Add the chile and sauté for about 2 minutes until softened and beginning to brown.

3. Add the guanciale strips and fry for about 5 minutes until golden brown.

4. Stir in the tomatoes, turn the heat to low, and cook for 10 minutes until the sauce thickens slightly.

5. Taste and season with salt and pepper.

6. Stir in the cheese. If the sauce is for pasta, add the cheese after dressing the pasta.

PANCETTA AND SPINACH SAUCE

1. Prepare an ice bath.

2. Bring a saucepan full of water to a boil. Add the spinach and blanch for 1 minute. Drain, transfer to the ice bath to stop the cooking, then drain again. Transfer the spinach to food processor or blender, or a medium bowl and use an immersion blender, and blend until creamy, adding a little water as needed.

3. Pour a few swirls of oil into a skillet and add the garlic and chile. Sauté over medium heat for about 3 minutes until softened and beginning to brown.

4. Turn the heat to high and add the pancetta. Sauté for 2 minutes, or until it begins to crisp around the edges.

5. Stir in the puréed spinach and soffrito. Sauté for 5 minutes to heat through.

6. Taste and season with salt and pepper.

Yield: 4 servings

1 pound (454 g) fresh spinach

Olive oil

1 garlic clove, peeled and minced

1 fresh chile pepper (such as serrano or jalapeño), destemmed, seeded and minced

8 ounces (225 g) pancetta or bacon, diced

2 tablespoons (16 g) Soffrito (page 11)

Salt and fresh-cracked black pepper

BEST ON:
- Cooked pasta (all types)

GOES WELL ON:
- Boiled potatoes
- Bruschetta and crostini
- Crespelle
- Eggs
- Gnocchi
- Rice and risotto
- Stuffed pasts (cheese, meat, or vegetables)

RED SAUCE WITH PANCETTA AND OLIVES

Yield: 4 servings

1 tablespoon (15 ml) olive oil

8 ounces (225 g) pancetta or bacon, diced

1 fresh red chile pepper (such as a Fresno chile), destemmed, seeded and diced, or 1 teaspoon red pepper flakes

1½ cups (270 g) fresh San Marzano or Roma tomatoes, seeded coarsely chopped

1½ cups (150 g) pitted black olives

¼ cup (33 g) Soffrito (page 11)

Salt and fresh-cracked black pepper

BEST ON:
- Al dente pasta

GOES WELL ON:
- Boiled potatoes
- Bruschetta and crostini
- Crespelle
- Eggs
- Gnocchi
- Polenta

1. In a skillet over medium-high heat, heat the oil until it shimmers. Add the pancetta and chile. Sauté for 3 to 4 minutes until the pancetta begins to brown and the chile softens.

2. Stir in the tomatoes, olives, soffrito. Turn the heat to low and cook for 10 minutes, stirring occasionally, until heated through and slightly thickened.

3. Taste and season with salt and pepper.

GRICIA SAUCE

1. Pour a few generous swirls of oil into a skillet and add the onion and guanciale. Sauté over medium heat for 5 to 7 minutes, or until browned and the onion is translucent. Remove the skillet from the heat and add a little water to deglaze the skillet, scraping up any browned bits from the bottom.

2. Taste and season generously with pepper.

3. Stir in the cheese at the last moment before serving. If the sauce is for pasta, add the cheese after dressing the pasta.

Yield: 4 servings

Olive oil

1 large onion, chopped

8 ounces (225 g) guanciale, pancetta, or bacon, cut into small strips

Fresh-cracked black pepper

6 ounces (172 g) grated grana (such as Asiago, Parmigiano-Reggiano, or Pecorino Romano)

BEST ON:
- Al dente pasta
- Bruschetta and crostini

GOES WELL ON:
- Boiled potatoes
- Crespelle
- Eggs
- Gnocchi
- Pizza, focaccia, piadina
- Polenta

CLASSIC CARBONARA

Yield: 4 to 6 servings

About 5 ounces (140 g) guanciale, pancetta, or bacon, diced

5 large egg yolks

About 5 ounces (140 g) grated grana (such as Asiago, Parmigiano-Reggiano, or Pecorino Romano)

Fresh-cracked black pepper

BEST ON:
- Al dente pasta

GOES WELL ON:
- Gnocchi

1. Place the guanciale in a nonstick skillet over high heat. Sauté for 2 to 3 minutes, or until it begins to render its fat and is cooked to your liking.

2. In a large bowl, whisk the egg yolks while adding the cheese a bit at a time until blended and combined.

3. Generously season with pepper and whisk to combine.

4. When dressing the hot pasta with the sauce, which will cook the eggs gently from its residual heat, add about ½ cup (120 ml) of the pasta cooking water, as needed, for a creamier texture, and the guanciale and stir gently to coat and combine. If you're concerned about uncooked egg, combine everything in the skillet and cook gently over low heat for about 1 minute, stirring constantly, to cook the egg.

SAUSAGE AND BROCCOLI RABE SAUCE

1. Remove the sausage from its casing and chop it.

2. Clean the broccoli rabe by removing the stems and detaching the tops. Mince the inner part of the tops and chop the rest.

3. Pour a few swirls of oil into a saucepan and add the garlic, chile, and minced broccoli rabe tops. Sauté over medium heat for about 5 minutes until the vegetables soften and begin to brown.

4. Add the chopped broccoli rabe pieces, soffrito, and the sausage. Cook for 5 minutes, stirring, or until the vegetables are tender and the sausage is browned and cooked through (no pink remains).

5. Taste and season with salt and pepper.

Yield: 4 to 6 servings

12 ounces (340 g) sweet Italian sausage, chopped

2 pounds (908 g) broccoli rabe (cime di rapa)

Olive oil

1 garlic clove, peeled and minced

1 fresh chile pepper (such as serrano or jalapeño), destemmed, seeded and minced

¼ cup (33 g) Soffrito (page 11)

Salt and fresh-cracked black pepper

BEST ON:
- Cooked pasta (any type)

GOES WELL ON:
- Boiled potatoes
- Gnocchi
- Pizza, focaccia, piadina
- Rice and risotto
- Stuffed pasta (cheese or vegetables)

SAUSAGE AND ToMATO SAUCE

Yield: 4 servings

1 pound (454 g) fresh San Marzano or Roma tomatoes, or 1 (14.5-ounce, or 410 g) can whole peeled San Marzano tomatoes

1 tablespoon (14 g) lard or butter

1 fresh red chile pepper (such as a Fresno chile), destemmed, seeded and chopped, or 1 teaspoon red pepper flakes

8 ounces (225 g) Italian sausage, chopped

¼ cup (33 g) Soffrito (page 11)

BEST ON:
- Cooked pasta (all types)
- Lasagna and cannelloni
- Stuffed pasta (cheese, meat, or vegetables)

GOES WELL ON:
- Boiled potatoes
- Bruschetta and crostini
- Crespelle
- Eggs
- Gnocchi
- Pizza, focaccia, piadina
- Polenta

1. If using fresh tomatoes, prepare an ice bath. Score the tomatoes with an X on the bottom to make them easier to peel. Bring a large pot of water to a boil, add the tomatoes, and cook for about 1 minute, or until the skins start to peel back in the place where you scored them. Using a slotted spoon, transfer the tomatoes to the ice bath. When cool enough to handle, peel the tomatoes, halve them, remove the seeds, and coarsely chop them.

2. In a skillet over high heat, melt the lard. Add the chile and sausage pieces and sauté for 5 minutes until the sausage begins to brown.

3. Stir in the tomatoes and soffrito. Turn the heat to low and cook for 10 minutes, stirring occasionally, until the sausage is cooked through (no pink remains) and the sauce has thickened slightly.

SAUSAGE AND FRIARIELLI SAUCE

Yield: 4 servings

12 ounces (340 g) sweet Italian sausage, chopped

Olive oil

1 garlic clove, peeled and chopped

Salt and fresh-cracked black pepper

1 pound (454 g) broccoli friarielli (broccoli rabe), trimmed and coarsely chopped

1 fresh chile pepper (such as serrano or jalapeño), destemmed, seeded and chopped

¼ cup (33 g) Soffrito (page 11)

1. Place the chopped sausage in a skillet. Pour in a few swirls of oil and sauté over medium heat for 7 to 8 minutes, stirring occasionally, until browned. Sprinkle in the garlic and cook for about 30 seconds until fragrant.

2. Meanwhile, bring a medium-size saucepan full of generously salted water to a boil. Add the friarielli and cook for 3 to 4 minutes, or until tender. Drain and transfer to a food processor or blender, or a bowl and use an immersion blender. Add the chile pepper and soffrito and blend until smooth and creamy. Add the puréed vegetables to the sausage and stir to combine. Cook for 1 to 2 minutes until heated through.

3. Taste and season with salt and pepper.

BEST ON:
- Al dente pasta

GOES WELL ON:
- Boiled potatoes
- Bruschetta and crostini
- Cooked pasta (all types)
- Gnocchi
- Pizza, focaccia, piadina
- Polenta
- Rice and risotto
- Stewed legumes
- Stuffed pasta (cheese, meat, or vegetables)
- Veloutés and cream soups

MONZESE SAUCE

1. In a medium bowl, combine the dried mushrooms with enough water to cover. Let soak for about 20 minutes. Drain the mushrooms through a fine-mesh sieve set over a bowl, reserving the soaking liquid. Squeeze the excess water from the mushrooms into the bowl. Chop the mushrooms.

2. In a skillet over low heat, melt the butter. Add the onion and cook over for about 10 minutes, stirring occasionally, to sweat the onion until it is soft and translucent.

3. Dust the sausage with flour, tossing to coat, and add it to the skillet. Turn the heat to medium-high and sauté for 2 to 3 minutes so it begins to brown.

4. Pour in the wine to deglaze the skillet, scraping up any browned bits. Turn the heat to medium and simmer for about 3 minutes until the wine evaporates.

5. Stir in the tomato purée, soffrito, and the chopped mushrooms and their soaking liquid. Turn the heat to low and cook slowly for 30 minutes until the sauce is thickened and heated through.

6. Taste and season with salt and pepper.

4 ounces (115 g) dried porcini mushrooms

4 tablespoons (56 g) butter

1 white onion, finely sliced

About 10 ounces (280 g) Italian sausage, cut into small pieces

All-purpose flour for dusting

¼ cup (60 ml) white wine

1 cup (250 g) tomato purée

2 tablespoons (16 g) Soffrito (page 11)

Salt and fresh-cracked black pepper

BEST ON:
- Al dente penne (or other ridged pasta)
- Polenta

GOES WELL ON:
- Boiled potatoes
- Bruschetta and crostini
- Eggs
- Gnocchi
- Lasagna and cannelloni
- Polenta
- Rice and risotto
- Stewed legumes

SAUSAGE AND ARTICHOKE SAUCE

Yield: 4 to 6 servings

Juice of 1 lemon

6 artichokes

Olive oil

2 garlic cloves, peeled and minced

1 cup (240 ml) vegetable broth

About 10 ounces (280 g) sweet Italian sausage, chopped

Salt and fresh-cracked black pepper

1 bunch fresh parsley, chopped

BEST ON:
- Bruschetta and crostini
- Cooked pasta (all types)
- Pizza

GOES WELL ON:
- Boiled potatoes
- Cooked meats (hot or cold)
- Gnocchi
- Lasagna and cannelloni
- Stuffed pasta (cheese, meat, or vegetables)

1. Fill a large bowl with water and stir in the lemon juice.

2. Cut off the stems from the artichokes, peel them, and cut the stems into thin slices. Soak the stems in the acidulated lemon water until ready to use.

3. Remove the outer leaves from the artichokes and cut off the tips. Halve the artichokes, then quarter them. Remove the barbs and cut the quarters into pieces. Add them to the lemon water.

4. Pour a few swirls of oil into a nonstick skillet and add the garlic. Sauté over medium heat for about 30 seconds until fragrant.

5. Drain the artichokes and add them to the skillet. Pour in the broth, turn the heat to low, and simmer until tender. Transfer half of the artichokes to a food processor or blender, or to a medium-size bowl and use an immersion blender, and blend until smooth. Transfer the remaining artichokes into a bowl.

6. Return the skillet to the stovetop and add the sausage, increase the heat to medium-high, and sauté for about 5 minutes, or until browned. Stir in the puréed artichokes and remaining cooked artichokes.

7. Taste and season with salt and pepper, then sprinkle with plenty of chopped parsley.

VALDOSTANA CARBONADE

1. In a saucepan over medium heat, melt the butter. Add the onion and cook for 3 to 5 minutes until softened and beginning to brown.

2. Add the veal and cook for about 2 minutes, turning once, just until browned.

3. Pour in the wine to deglaze the pan, scraping up any browned bits from the bottom. Simmer for about 3 minutes until the wine evaporates.

4. Sprinkle the flour over everything. Add the sage and a pinch of nutmeg. Pour in enough water to cover and let cook for 1 hour until the sauce has thickened and the veal is tender.

5. Taste and season with salt and pepper.

Yield: 4 to 6 servings

1 tablespoon (14 g) butter

1 red onion, chopped

1½ pounds (683 g) veal filet, cut into small pieces

½ cup (120 ml) white wine

1 tablespoon (7.5 g) all-purpose flour

3 fresh sage leaves

Freshly grated nutmeg for seasoning

Salt and fresh-cracked black pepper

BEST ON:
- Bruschetta and crostini
- Cooked pasta (all types)
- Polenta

GOES WELL ON:
- Crespelle
- Gnocchi
- Lasagna and cannelloni
- Rice and risotto
- Stuffed pasta (cheese, meat, or vegetables)

CREAM SAUCE WITH PEAS AND HAM

Yield: 4 to 6 servings

1 pound (454 g) shelled
   peas, fresh or frozen
   and thawed

3½ tablespoons (49 g) butter

⅓ cup (36 g) potato starch

2½ cups (600 ml) heavy cream

About 10 ounces (280 g)
   cooked ham in a single
   slice, diced

Salt and fresh-cracked
   black pepper

BEST ON:
- Cooked pasta (all types)

GOES WELL ON:
- Boiled potatoes
- Cooked meats (hot)
- Gnocchi
- Lasagna and cannelloni
- Pasta salad
- Rice and risotto
- Stuffed pasta (cheese,
  meat, or vegetables)

1. Bring a saucepan full of water to a boil. Add the peas and blanch for 1 minute. Drain and rinse with cool water to stop the cooking. Drain again.

2. Return the saucepan to low heat and add the butter to melt.

3. Add the potato starch slowly, stirring with a wooden spoon to coat the starch with the butter.

4. While stirring constantly, trickle in the cream until it's combined with the roux. Cook over low heat for about 10 minutes, stirring, until the sauce has thickened.

5. Stir in the diced ham and peas. Cook for about 2 minutes to heat through.

6. Taste and season with salt and pepper.

LE VIRTÙ SAUCE

Yield: 6 to 8 servings

2 cups (500 g) mixed dried legumes, rinsed and picked over for debris

1 bunch fresh spinach, coarsely chopped

1 bunch fresh chard, coarsely chopped

1 carrot, coarsely chopped

1 onion, coarsely chopped

1 celery stalk, coarsely chopped

1 fennel bulb, coarsely chopped

Olive oil

1 pound (454 g) pork, chopped

4 cups (960 ml) beef stock, plus more as needed

Salt and fresh-cracked black pepper

BEST ON:
- Cooked pasta (all types, especially small shapes like ditalini and macaroni)

GOES WELL ON:
- Boiled potatoes
- Bruschetta and crostini
- Polenta
- Rice and risotto

1. In a large pot, combine the dried legumes with enough water to cover by a few inches. Let soak overnight. Drain and wipe the pot dry.

2. Add the spinach, chard, carrot, onion, celery, and fennel to the pot. Pour in a few generous swirls of oil and sauté over medium heat for 5 to 7 minutes, or until the vegetables begin to soften.

3. Add the chopped pork to the vegetables.

4. Stir in the legumes, pour in the stock (adding more if the ingredients are not covered), and turn the heat to low. Simmer for 3 hours. You should have a fairly dry preparation.

5. Taste and season with salt and pepper.

PORK RIB SAUCE

Yield: 4 to 6 servings

1. In a Dutch oven over medium-high heat, combine the ribs, tomato pulp, soffrito, onion, basil leaves, and chile.

2. In a small bowl, stir together the tomato paste and water until the tomato paste dissolves. Stir the mixture into the pot. Bring to a boil, cover the pot, turn the heat to low, and simmer for about 3 hours, stirring occasionally and adding a bit more water if the sauce become dry, or until the sauce is thickened and the meat falls off the bones.

3. Remove the bones from the pork rib and strip them of any remaining meat. Chop the meat and put it back into the sauce, breaking it up if desired. Discard the bones.

4. Taste and season with salt and pepper.

1½ pounds (681 g) pork ribs

2½ cups (625 g) tomato pulp or crushed tomatoes in purée

¼ cup (33 g) Soffrito (page 11)

1 white onion, sliced

1 bunch fresh basil

1 fresh chile pepper (such as serrano or jalapeño), destemmed, seeded and chopped

½ cup (130 g) tomato paste

1 cup (240 ml) water

Salt and fresh-cracked black pepper

BEST ON:
- Cooked pasta (all types, especially egg pasta)

GOES WELL ON:
- Boiled potatoes
- Bruschetta and crostini
- Cooked meats (hot)
- Gnocchi
- Lasagna and cannelloni
- Polenta
- Stuffed pasta (cheese, meat, or vegetables)

LAMB AND PORCINI MUSHROOM SAUCE

Yield: 6 servings

12 ounces (340 g) fresh porcini mushrooms, trimmed and diced

1 red onion, diced

1 celery stalk, diced

1 large carrot, diced

1 bunch fresh parsley, chopped

Olive oil

1½ pounds (681 g) ground lamb

½ cup (120 ml) white wine

¼ cup (33 g) Soffrito (page 11)

½ cup (120 ml) water

Salt and fresh-cracked black pepper

1. Add the onion, celery, carrot, and parsley to a saucepan. Pour in a few swirls of oil and sauté over medium heat for 3 to 5 minutes until the vegetables begin to soften and brown.

2. Add the ground lamb, turn the heat to high, and sauté for 5 minutes until the lamb is no longer pink.

3. Pour in the wine to deglaze the pan, scraping up any browned bits from the bottom. Simmer for about 3 minutes until the wine evaporates.

4. Stir in the mushrooms and soffrito. Add the water, turn the heat to low, and cook for 30 minutes until the sauce is thickened, stirring occasionally and adding more water if the sauce becomes dry.

5. Taste and season with salt and pepper.

BEST ON:
- Cooked pasta (all types, especially egg pasta)
- Lasagna and cannelloni

GOES WELL ON:
- Bruschetta and crostini
- Eggs
- Gnocchi
- Polenta
- Rice and risotto
- Stewed legumes
- Stuffed pasta (cheese, meat, or vegetables)

SPICY BEEF SAUCE

1. Saute the beef in olive oil in a saucepan over medium heat until it is cooked through, about 5 minutes. Reduce the heat to low and add the wine, vinegar, soffrito, thyme, and bay leaves. Cook over low heat until the wine has reduced by about half. Remove and discard the bay leaves.

2. Pour in the stock and season the sauce generously with cayenne. Simmer for a few minutes more to warm through and thicken slightly.

3. Strain the sauce through a fine-mesh sieve set over a heatproof bowl. Discard the solids.

4. Taste and season the sauce with salt.

Yield: 4 to 6 servings

½ pound (227 g) finely chopped beef, such as chuck or sirloin

Olive oil

1 cup (240 ml) dry white wine

½ cup (120 ml) apple cider vinegar

¼ cup (33 g) Soffrito (page 11)

2 thyme sprigs

2 bay leaves

1 cup (240 ml) beef stock

Cayenne pepper for seasoning

Salt

BEST ON:
- Cooked meats (hot, especially grilled)
- Stuffed pasta (cheese, meat, or vegetables)

GOES WELL ON:
- Boiled potatoes
- Gnocchi
- Rice and risotto

ROASTED BEEF SAUCE

Yield: 4 servings

3 tablespoons (21 g) butter

1 rosemary sprig

1 garlic clove, peeled

About 10 ounces (280 g) leftover roasted beef, or deli roast beef, finely chopped

½ cup (120 ml) port or Marsala wine

¼ cup (33 g) Soffrito (page 11)

Salt and fresh-cracked black pepper

BEST ON:
- Al dente pasta
- Bruschetta and crostini

GOES WELL ON:
- Crespelle
- Gnocchi
- Lasagna and cannelloni
- Polenta
- Pizza, focaccia, piadina
- Pasta salad
- Stuffed pasta (cheese, meat, or vegetables)

1. In a skillet over medium heat, combine the butter, rosemary, and garlic. Heat until the butter melts and the garlic is fragrant.

2. Add the chopped beef and sauté for 2 to 3 minutes, or until well browned.

3. Pour in the wine to deglaze the skillet, scraping up any browned bits from the bottom. Simmer for about 3 minutes until the wine evaporates.

4. Stir in the soffrito and cook for 3 minutes more, stirring. Remove and discard the garlic and rosemary.

5. Taste and season with salt and pepper.

CARRETTIERA SAUCE

1. Pour a few swirls of oil into a saucepan and add the beef. Cook over medium-high heat for about 5 minutes, stirring occasionally, or until the beef is browned. Add the garlic and sauté for 30 seconds to 1 minute until fragrant and beginning to soften.

2. Pour in the wine to deglaze the pan, scraping up any browned bits from the bottom. Turn the heat to medium and simmer for about 3 minutes until the wine evaporates.

3. In a small bowl, stir together the tomato paste and water until the tomato paste dissolves, then add the mixture to the skillet, along with the soffrito, and stir to combine. Cook for 30 minutes, adding a little hot water if the sauce becomes dry.

4. Stir the parsley into the sauce.

5. Taste and season with salt and the red pepper flakes. Remove and discard the garlic.

Yield: 4 servings

Olive oil

1 pound (454 g) well-marbled beef (such as chuck rib-eye roast), diced with a chef's knife

1 large garlic clove, crushed

½ cup (120 ml) red or white wine

1 tablespoon (15 g) tomato paste

½ cup (120 ml) water

6 tablespoons (46 g) Soffrito (page 11)

1 bunch fresh parsley, chopped

Salt

1 teaspoon red pepper flakes

BEST ON:
- Cooked pasta (all types)
- Polenta
- Stuffed pasta (cheese, meat, or vegetables)

GOES WELL ON:
- Boiled potatoes
- Bruschetta and crostini
- Crespelle
- Eggs
- Gnocchi
- Lasagna and cannelloni
- Pizza, focaccia, piadina
- Rice and risotto

MARENGO SAUCE

Yield: 6 to 8 servings

Type "00" flour or all-purpose flour for coating

1 pound (454 g) boneless, skinless chicken breast, cut into bite-size pieces

2 garlic cloves, peeled and finely chopped

Olive oil

½ cup (120 ml) white wine

2½ cups (625 g) tomato purée

About 10 ounces (280 g) champignon (white button) mushrooms, trimmed and diced

Juice of 1 lemon

12 shrimp, peeled, deveined, and chopped

Salt and fresh-cracked black pepper

1 bunch fresh parsley, chopped

1. Place some flour in a medium-size bowl. Add the pieces of chicken to the flour, and toss to coat.

2. Pour a few swirls of oil into a saucepan and add the coated chicken and garlic. Sauté over medium heat for about 5 minutes until the chicken is lightly browned.

3. Pour the wine into the pan to deglaze it, scraping up any browned bits from the bottom.

4. Stir in the tomato purée, turn the heat to high, and cook for 10 minutes, stirring occasionally.

5. Add the mushrooms to the chicken and cook for 10 minutes more, stirring occasionally.

6. Stir in the lemon juice and chopped shrimp. Cook for 1 to 2 minutes until the shrimp turn pink and are cooked through and opaque.

7. Taste and season with salt and pepper, then sprinkle with plenty of chopped parsley.

BEST ON:
- Cooked pasta (all types)
- Gnocchi
- Polenta

GOES WELL ON:
- Boiled potatoes
- Bruschetta and crostini
- Crespelle
- Lasagna and cannelloni
- Pizza, focaccia, piadina
- Rice and risotto

CHICKEN MEATBALLS IN TOMATO SAUCE

1. Add the garlic to a saucepan. Pour in a few swirls of oil and sauté over medium heat for about 30 seconds until fragrant.

2. Pour in the tomato purée, turn the heat to low, and simmer for 15 minutes.

3. Meanwhile, in a small bowl, soak the bread pieces in enough milk to cover.

4. Pour the bread crumbs into a shallow bowl and set aside.

5. Place the chopped rosemary in a medium-size bowl. Add the ground chicken and egg. Squeeze the milk from the bread and add the soaked bread to the bowl. Season with salt and pepper. Using your hands, mix everything together, then form the mixture into small (1-inch, or 2.5 cm) meatballs. Dip the meatballs in the bread crumbs to coat and place on a plate.

6. In a skillet over medium heat, heat about 1 inch (2.5 cm) of oil until shimmering. Carefully add the chicken meatballs to the hot oil and cook for 2 to 3 minutes per side until browned all over and cooked through (no pink remains). Transfer the chicken meatballs to the saucepan with the tomato sauce and cook for 5 minutes to heat and combine.

7. Taste and season with salt and pepper.

Yield: 4 to 6 servings

2 garlic cloves, peeled and chopped

Olive oil

4 cups (1 kg) tomato purée

1 cup (50 g) torn soft bread pieces

Milk for soaking

1⅔ cups (192 g) bread crumbs

1 rosemary sprig, finely chopped with stem removed

1 pound (454 g) ground chicken

1 egg

Salt and fresh-cracked black pepper

BEST ON:
- Cooked pasta (all types)
- Gnocchi

GOES WELL ON:
- Boiled potatoes
- Crespelle
- Lasagna and cannelloni
- Pizza, focaccia, piadina
- Polenta
- Rice and risotto
- Stewed legumes
- Stuffed pasta (cheese or vegetables)

8
THE
BASICS

MY SIGNATURE SEASONED BUTTER

Yield: 12 servings
(1 tablespoon, or 14 g each)

2 garlic cloves, peeled
  and chopped

1 shallot, chopped

½ cup (120 ml) dry white wine

12 tablespoons (1½ sticks,
  or 168 g) butter, at room
  temperature

Juice of 1 lemon

1 bunch fresh parsley,
  chopped

Mustard of choice for
  seasoning

Salt and fresh-cracked
  black pepper

BEST ON:
- Al dente pasta
- Cooked meats and fish (hot)
- Grilled meat

GOES WELL ON:
- Boiled potatoes
- Bruschetta and crostini
- Cooked vegetables
- Crustaceans
- Gnocchi
- Polenta
- Rice and risotto

1. Place the garlic and shallot in a small saucepan. Pour in the wine and cook over medium heat for about 3 minutes, or until the wine evaporates completely. Let cool.

2. Stir in the butter, lemon juice, parsley, a touch of mustard, and salt and pepper to taste until well mixed. Transfer the butter mixture to a piece of plastic wrap and roll it into a cylindrical shape. Refrigerate until needed.

3. When the dish is ready and hot, cut a pat of seasoned butter and place it on top to slowly melt.

CREAM SAUCE

1. In a saucepan over low heat, melt the butter.

2. Add the potato starch slowly, stirring with a wooden spoon to coat the starch with the butter.

3. While stirring constantly, trickle in the cream until it's combined with the roux. Cook over low heat for about 10 minutes, stirring, until the sauce has thickened.

4. Taste and season with salt.

Yield: 4 to 6 servings

3½ tablespoons (49 g) butter

⅓ cup (36 g) potato starch

2½ cups (600 ml) heavy cream

Salt

BEST ON:
- Boiled potatoes
- Cooked pasta (all types)
- Cooked beef fillet (hot or cold)

GOES WELL ON:
- Cooked vegetables
- Crespelle
- Gnocchi
- Lasagna and cannelloni
- Raw meats and fish: tartare and carpaccio

GARLIC, OIL, AND CHILE SAUCE

Yield: 4 servings

½ cup (120 ml) olive oil

6 large garlic cloves, peeled and finely chopped

1 fresh chile pepper (such as serrano or jalapeño), destemmed, seeded, and diced

Salt and fresh-cracked black pepper

BEST ON:
- Al dente pasta
- Cooked vegetables
- Veloutés and cream soups

GOES WELL ON:
- Boiled potatoes
- Bruschetta and crostini
- Cooked meats and fish (hot or cold)
- Crustaceans
- Gnocchi
- Pizza, focaccia, piadina
- Raw meats and fish: tartare and carpaccio
- Stewed legumes

1. Pour the oil into a skillet and add the garlic and chile. Cook the vegetables over low heat for about 3 minutes, or until the garlic is golden and fragrant and the chile is softened, being careful not to burn the garlic or your sauce will taste bitter.

2. Taste and season with salt and pepper.

3. When dressing the pasta with the sauce, add about ½ cup (120 ml) of the pasta cooking water for a creamier result.

MORNAY SAUCE

2 cups (500 g) béchamel sauce, homemade or store-bought

1 cup (240 ml) heavy cream

4 ounces (115 g) grated grana (such as Asiago, Parmigiano-Reggiano, or Pecorino Romano)

Salt and fresh-cracked black pepper

¼ cup (68 g) egg yolks

BEST ON:
- Cooked pasta (any type)
- Cooked vegetables
- Roasted beef

GOES WELL ON:
- Boiled potatoes
- Crespelle
- Eggs
- Gnocchi
- Lasagna and cannelloni
- Polenta
- Stuffed pasta (cheese, meat, seafood, or vegetables)

1. In a saucepan over very low heat, gently warm the béchamel.

2. While whisking constantly, slowly add the cream, grana, and pepper to taste. Cook, whisking, until the cheese melts into the sauce and thickens it.

3. Remove from the heat and gently whisk in the egg yolks until emulsified. The residual heat of the sauce will cook the eggs gently; If you're concerned about uncooked egg, after adding the yolks, cook the sauce gently over low heat for about 1 minute, stirring constantly.

4. Taste and season with salt.

SMETANA SAUCE

1. In a large bowl, whisk the sour cream and lemon juice until emulsified.

2. Season with a pinch of salt and paprika to taste and whisk to combine.

3. In a saucepan over low heat, melt the butter.

4. In small bowl, stir together the tomato paste and water until the tomato paste dissolve, then whisk it into the butter.

5. Whisk in the sour cream and cook over low heat for about 8 minutes until heated through, stirring occasionally.

Yield: 4 to 6 servings

2½ cups (575 g) sour cream

Juice of 1 lemon, strained

Salt

Paprika for seasoning

1½ tablespoons (21 g) butter

¼ cup (60 g) tomato paste

½ cup (120 ml) water

BEST ON:
- Cooked meats (hot or cold)

GOES WELL ON:
- Boiled potatoes
- Cooked fish (hot or cold)
- Cooked vegetables
- Pasta salad
- Raw meats and fish: tartare and carpaccio
- Stewed legumes

ABOUT THE AUTHOR

ALLAN BAY is a tremendously popular and well-respected food historian, cooking teacher, translator, and writer who specializes in the regional and national cuisines of Italy. His series of Italian cookbooks for beginners, *Cuochi si Diventa* ("You Can Become a Cook"), is a perennial best-seller in Italy and in translated editions around the world. He has written fifteen other highly admired cookbooks. He lives and writes in Rome.

INDEX